WORSHIP OR ENTERTAINMENT?

WORSHIP OR ENTERTAINMENT?

PETER MASTERS

THE WAKEMAN TRUST * LONDON

WORSHIP OR ENTERTAINMENT?
© Peter Masters
First published under the title *Worship in the Melting Pot,* 2002
This revised and condensed edition 2020

THE WAKEMAN TRUST
(Wakeman Trust is a UK Registered Charity)

Wakeman Trust UK Registered Office
38 Walcot Square
London SE11 4TZ

Wakeman Trust USA Office
300 Artino Drive
Oberlin, OH 44074-1263
Website: www.wakemantrust.org

ISBN 978 1 913133 05 4

Cover design by Andrew Owen

Printed by Stephens & George, Merthyr Tydfil, UK

CONTENTS

'God is a Spirit: and they that worship him must worship him in spirit and in truth' *(John 4.24).*

CHAPTER 1

Is it Worship or Entertainment?

O UR MANNER OF WORSHIP is one of the most important issues confronting Bible churches today, and here is
why. Six highly flawed styles of worship may be observed – often
all mixed together. There is *personal-pleasure worship*, which puts
the worshipper's enjoyment in first place, rather than God's desire.
There is *worldly-idiom worship*, which borrows the current entertainment music of the world with its rhythms, instruments, actions
and showbiz presentation, heedless of all the Bible's warnings
about loving the world. There is *aesthetic worship*, which imagines
that orchestras, bands and instrumental solos are real expressions
of worship, as if God is worshipped *through* these things, whereas
Christ said – 'God is a Spirit: and they that worship him must
worship him in spirit and in truth.' There is *ecstatic worship*, in
which people work themselves into highly emotional and even semi-
hypnotic states, whereas Scripture says that we must always pray and
sing with the understanding. There is *shallow worship*, which reduces
hymns to choruses conveying one or two elementary ideas, because

solid spiritual themes are not wanted. There is *informal worship*, in which casual, jokey, trivia-injecting leaders turn churches into sitting rooms, so depriving the Lord of dignity, reverence, grandeur and glory.

It is as though Bible-believing churches have caught six viruses at the same time. How can churches survive in the power of the Spirit if their highest occupation is sick? How can God's people keep themselves unspotted from the world, if the world has taken over the worship? How can we call lost souls out of the world, if we are the same as the world? Worship is certainly among the most important topics of the hour.

In this book I would like to speak with great respect to fellow Christians, including pastors and church officers, who have adopted elements of contemporary worship. They have been persuaded that their reservations are merely a matter of taste and culture, and that they should introduce some of the new alongside the old, thus preserving the best of traditional worship. The problem with this is that the old and the new represent opposing concepts of worship, as these pages will show. The new breaks all the biblical principles recovered at the Reformation. Even the history of new worship rings alarm bells, and demonstrates the chasm between the old and the new.

The development of new worship is now fairly well known, and can be sketched here in a few sentences. It mainly began in California in the late 1960s, when many hippies turned to Christ, becoming known as the 'Jesus people'. They worshipped with the very same style of song which they had known as hippies. Various Christian movements were formed to encourage them, among them the well-known Calvary Chapels. Their worship consisted mostly of one-verse choruses, endlessly repeated. The words were simple – simpler even than those of a traditional children's chorus. There was seldom any confession of sin or the expression of any doctrine. However well-intended, the new worship was not shaped or influenced by any biblical model of worship, nor by the general practice of Bible-believing churches up to that time.

It was a form of worship fashioned and conceived in the womb of meditational mysticism, in which hippies in their hundreds and thousands would sit on Californian hillsides with eyes closed, swaying themselves into an ecstatic state, echoing their previous experience with drugs. Former hippies carried into their new Christian allegiance the same quest for emotional sensation to which they were accustomed, and, sadly, none of their Christian mentors showed them a better way.

This new approach to worship rapidly advanced, merging with another new stream of 'Christian' songs written by those who simply wanted worship music to be like secular rock music. In other words, the latter wanted a 'good time' in a worldly sense. We need to be aware that new worship sprang from these two stables, namely, hippie mysticism and worldly Christianity. It was rapidly incorporated into the charismatic movement, from which the vast majority of new worship songs have come. Some years later, during the late 1980s, many sounder, more biblical churches began to adopt the new worship styles.

Such background information should lead us to great caution, but the *biblical principles* of the following pages should be the decisive factor in whether we accept or reject the new ways. We surely cannot blend opposing concepts. Is it worship or entertainment? – this is the question.

'Contemporary Christian music' has now captured countless congregations of every theological hue throughout the world, though not without many a battle. As a rule the chief strategy employed by the advocates of new worship has been to reduce the entire debate to a matter of taste, style and generation.

Those who keep to the 'old' ways are sometimes charged with a selfish refusal to adjust to changing culture. They have even been called the Pharisees of the 21st-century church, guilty of obstructing a great forward movement of God's people and forcing division over non-essentials. For all this, large numbers of churches throughout the world still resist the new ways, believing that great principles are at stake.

The trouble with the rhetoric of those advocating new worship is that they seem not to recognise, let alone discuss, historic, biblical principles of worship. It is as if there is nothing much about worship in the Bible. It is as if the Reformation never reformed worship back to the Scriptures. It is as though the bedrock definitions held over centuries have become invisible and non-existent. Where have these priceless and vital principles gone? Why are they hardly ever discussed? Do the advocates of new worship wilfully avoid them, or are they genuinely unaware of them? Certainly, it is an astonishing scene to find them passed over so easily.

The sixty-plus generation of believers remember that these principles were still being taught in their youth, but not any more. New definitions of worship have appeared which would never have been accepted as recently as fifty years ago – definitions which smash down the central principles of evangelical, Protestant Christian worship, taking us back to medieval and Catholic thinking. We will begin by identifying three major deviations from biblical standards (as recovered at the Reformation) typical of the entire modern worship movement. A fourth serious deviation appears in chapter 12.

Churches that have adopted modern worship songs and music to only a limited degree must take account of the deeply significant errors which govern the writers and composers of the new genre, most of whom embrace a shallow theology and hold ecumenical objectives.

CHAPTER 2

THREE BROKEN PRINCIPLES
I – Spiritual or Aesthetic Worship?

OUR FIRST MAJOR deviation is the adoption of *aesthetic worship*, in preference to the Lord's requirement that worship must exclusively be 'in spirit and in truth' (see *John 4.23-24*). 'In spirit' makes worship a product of heart and soul. Aesthetic worship, by contrast, is the idea that things that are beautiful, artistic or skilfully executed should be offered up as an expression of worship to God. It is based on the notion that we worship not just with spiritual thoughts from our minds and hearts, but also with the creative and instrumental skill of our minds and hands.

The exponents of aesthetic worship think that praise needs a 'physical' dimension greater than mere singing. They assume that God wants us to bring things of skill and beauty before him. We must bring thrilling music, clever arrangements, brilliant instrumentalism and fine singing, and these will please him. We may worship (it is thought) not only by meaningful words, but by performance.

This is of immense importance, because the *aesthetic* idea of worship is totally opposed to God's standards, and is the very essence of medieval Catholicism. The Church of Rome, with all her masses, images, processions, soaring naves, stained glass windows, costly and colourful robes, rich music, Gregorian chants, and complex proceedings, makes an offering of worship *by these things*. All her theatricalism is an act of worship believed to be pleasing to God. The spiritual giants of the Reformation turned back to the Bible, unitedly embracing the principle that true worship is intelligent (and scriptural) *words*, whether said, thought or sung, winged by faith to the Lord. It is true that little bits of Roman 'theatre' remained in the episcopal churches, but generally speaking the rites, ceremonies, images and everything else that represented a virtuous offering were swept away.

We believe that the Lord trusts us with music and also with instruments to accompany the singing of praise, but these cannot actually convey worship. They are secondary. They are not in the image of God, nor do they have souls, nor are they redeemed. Modern era hymnwriter Erik Routley was way off the mark when he penned the lines (which he meant to be taken literally) –

> *Joyfully, heartily, resounding!*
> *Let every instrument and voice…*
>
> *Trumpets and organs, set in motion*
> *Such sounds as make the heavens ring.*

An earlier Anglo-Catholic hymn (by Francis Pott) made the same aesthetic point in these words –

> *Craftsmen's art and music's measure,*
> *For thy pleasure all combine.*

The recently coined, popular statement that worship is 'a celebration in words and music' also breaches the Lord's key principle that worship should exclusively be – 'in spirit and in truth'. Words and thoughts are everything in worship. Music may only assist at a practical level; it cannot be used to express worship. To believe that it can is to fall into the Romish error of aesthetic worship. The singing of God's people should certainly be grand and glorious in terms of fervour and effort, but it is the words and the hearts of the worshippers that God desires. All unnecessary embellishment is an offence to him, firstly, because he has not commanded it; secondly, because it is an insolent 'improvement' on what he has laid down; and thirdly, because it is a powerful distraction to spiritual worship. Does this sound strange? It may do so today, but fifty years ago – and all the way back to the Reformation – practically every evangelical Christian would have believed this most clearly.

Aesthetic worship has now flooded into evangelical Protestant churches as people have been persuaded that they should express much of their worship via music and instrumentation, even through dance, other bodily movements and drama.

An advocate of the new ways has defined worship as 'a discovery of God's will through encounter and impact'. Not only is instrumental and song performance offered as a meritorious expression of worship, but many Christians claim some form of revelation from God from the very performance of it. This nonsense is seriously believed by some of the main architects and promoters of new worship. Do evangelicals who adopt their materials realise the deep mystical errors that lie behind them? To put it bluntly, aesthetic worship is a huge stride back to the mindset of Rome, and has no place in the true church of Jesus Christ. It challenges and spoils genuine worship, and is contrary to every praise instruction in the New Testament. When we evaluate new worship, we must do so in terms of those biblical principles recovered (by God's mercy) at the time of the Reformation, the first of these being that worship is spiritual, and not an aesthetic performance. At the Reformation, simplicity, intelligibility and fidelity to the Bible replaced the religious showmanship of Rome.

Why did all this take place? The advocates of new worship do not seem to know. They are aware that the Reformation changed *doctrinal teaching*, but they do not appear to know why it also changed the manner of worship. Do the new-worship promoters think it was just a 'generation thing'? Do they picture Luther, Calvin, and the Protestant martyrs as the youngsters who just wanted a new culture? Do they believe it was all a matter of taste? The truth is, of course, that the Reformers saw through the sensual worship of Rome and rejected artistic skill and beauty as a valid expression of worship. They rejected the 'working up' of supposed spiritual experience by things which entranced the eyes and the ears; but we will speak of these later.

How has it come about that evangelical Christians have adopted the idea that worship includes an offering of beauty and skill? The most obvious reason is that many churches have resorted to musical entertainment as *the* chief method of attracting outsiders, and this music has to be justified as part of the worship. Also, in the USA even the sounder theological seminaries and Christian colleges have greatly enlarged their music departments and courses for 'worship leaders'. Inevitably the role of music and the use of complex worship programmes has increased even in conservative circles. Many churches have acquired 'ministers of music' as well as professional worship leaders, and how could these highly trained people function if they did not feel that all their expertise and creativity somehow formed part of an efficacious offering of worship?

In biblical worship, only one offering counts, and that is the offering made once for all by the eternal Son of God on Calvary's cross. Nothing should be thought of as an acceptable offering, or as having any intrinsic merit, apart from Calvary. Our thoughts and words are not an 'offering', but expressions of praise, thanksgiving, repentance, supplication, dedication and obedience, all made acceptable by Calvary.

Writers promoting new worship often use language which depicts God as a satisfied viewer of a 'performance'. Some explicitly say that

God is the audience. In their books they provide illustrations of a stadium in which the church, with its choir and orchestra, are placed on the pitch, and the word 'God' is inscribed around the seating in the stands. They seem very pleased with this scenario.

Contemporary worship is fully aesthetic in purpose and practice. Skilful instrumentalism is considered a highly desirable part of the offering of worship. Churches today have gone blindly back to the philosophy of Rome, but they have far surpassed Rome in intricacy and decibel count. At the dawn of world history Abel's offering was accepted by the Lord because it was the specific act God had commanded – a humble offering representing the need for atonement. Cain's offering was rejected, because it presented his own skill, labour and artistry. It was a 'works' offering. To parade before God our skills as an act of worship is nearer to the offering of Cain than that of Abel.

We ask again, how is it that evangelicals have fallen into all this? We have not been helped by a number of practices which have served as the thin end of the aesthetic wedge. We have already observed that a few pre-Reformation features survived the Reformation – remnants of Catholic theatricalism, costumery and show. These have been kept up in Anglican churches (except in the 'low' churches), and they have always had an undermining effect, causing people to lose sight of a clear-cut definition of spiritual worship.

Inconsistent activities have also been adopted by nonconformist churches. Beautiful anthems rendered by choirs came to offer an increasingly aesthetic contribution to worship. Solo items in services introduced variety and seemed harmless enough, but they deepened the taste for novelties in worship. Then the solo often became an instrument-only item, so that congregations were given 'songs without words', and taught to regard these as acts of worship. Such practices helped erode away the biblical concept of worship, so that the Lord's people gradually lost sight of basic principles. By now, these principles have disappeared into oblivion.

It may be protested that worship in Old Testament times was rich in actions and artistry ordained by God, and such worship can hardly be disqualified. But it is not true that Old Testament services included works of beauty and skill as a direct expression of worship. The symbolism in the design of the Tabernacle and Temple, as well as the ceremonial performed by the priests, were prophecies in pictures of the work of Christ for them. These things amounted to *lessons*, not vehicles of worship. They served as visual sermons picturing the way of grace, not meritorious acts. The people observed and trusted, but their personal response of praise was intended to be spiritual and from the heart. True worship has always been a matter of the heart. We again urge readers to cleave to this central principle of worship, because how we worship is not just a matter of culture or taste or generation, but a matter of God-given rules. Principles count. The great statement common to the Westminster and Baptist confessions of the 17th century stands against all that has developed today:

> 'The acceptable way of worshipping the true God is instituted by himself, and so limited by his own revealed will, that he may not be worshipped according to the imagination and devices of men…'

It may help to conclude these pages on *Spiritual or Aesthetic Worship?* with a simple test question. Why would a church wish to increase or elaborate upon its customary instrumentation, and change its style of worship? If the answer is – 'To enrich our worship and to express our gifts' – then it will show that the principle of 'spirit and truth' has been lost, and the old aesthetic error has taken over.

CHAPTER 3

THREE BROKEN PRINCIPLES
II – Rational or Ecstatic Worship?

THE SECOND MAJOR deviation from biblical principles in contemporary worship is that it promotes a substitute for *rational*, intelligent worship which we will call *ecstatic* or emotional worship. The Lord requires us to worship him 'in spirit and in truth', the *truth* part meaning that worship must be from the conscious mind. Paul echoes this when he insists that Christians pray and sing with the understanding. The conscious, sound mind is the vital human organ of worship.*

Ecstatic worship is completely different. This aims at stirring the emotions to produce a highly emotional state, or a warm, happy feeling and great excitement. Earthly, physical elements of worship, such as music and movement, are employed to bring this about. The worship 'programme' is then engineered to bring worshippers to a high emotional pitch, even to a mildly hypnotic state. In

---

* See *1 Corinthians 14.15*, and chapter 5 – 'Let the Lord Define Worship'.

non-charismatic circles the objective is a little more modest, but essentially the same – to make an emotional impact. Worship leaders want to bypass rationality and get the feelings going by other means. They want to stir up 'sensations' to produce euphoria.

We do not accuse the advocates of new worship unfairly, because they say this themselves in their books and worship guides. The upbeat opening number will (they say) have such-and-such an effect upon worshippers, and then the music should take this or that direction to maintain the mood, and after that move to a lower tempo, volume and key, to stir different emotions. Instruments, arrangements, chords and beat should be woven into a pattern that will bend and sway the emotions of the people to maximise their sense of blessing.

Considerable musical expertise may go into the 'production' of a service, but any attempt to make a *direct* impression on the soul by the use of music or any other earthly tool is *ecstatic* worship as opposed to spiritual, rational worship. The latter does not try to manipulate the feelings, but derives its joy from sincere spiritual appreciation of the Lord, of his words, and of the great doctrines of the faith. Music (and instrumental accompaniment) is permitted by the Lord, but is not to be deliberately deployed as a means of arousing feelings. 'Feelings' in worship should be our genuine and voluntary response to things we understand and appreciate in our minds.

It is true that many hymn tunes touch our hearts because of their strong association with precious salvation words, and this is wholesome and acceptable. But the architects of ecstatic worship have no right to hijack this pleasant phenomenon, and to use music as the chief means of moving hearts and producing feelings. This is carnal, cynical, artificial and manipulative.

It is only as we are moved primarily by understandable thoughts providing a view of the Lord and his work, that we have genuine and legitimate spiritual feelings. Emotions fanned into flames by sentimental or stirring music may be enjoyable feelings at a purely human level, but they are not worship. The same goes for all artificially generated feelings. If a preacher moves people to weeping by telling 'tear-jerkers', their sense of need for God (or their repentance) will be nothing more than short-lived emotionalism. If, however, the people understand their need through hearing the Word (which is surely moving enough), their conviction and repentance will be genuine and lasting.

Music cannot really move the soul, but only the emotions. Valid worship always starts in the mind. If it is overwhelmed by the skilful and moving performance of a band or orchestra, it is compromised and spoiled. Such worship reminds us of the Israelites who desperately wanted to supplement manna with other foods. Today many say to God (in effect): 'You are not enough; I need unusually loud or rhythmic music in addition to excite me.'

Paul states a prime rule of worship in these words: 'Let all things be done unto edifying' (see *1 Corinthians 14.26*). The word *edifying* refers literally to the construction of a building, and Paul uses it to mean the building up of the understanding. Every element of worship must be understood in order to be valid. We are spiritually moved, not by melody, beauty or spectacle, but by what we understand. 'Worship,' says Puritan Stephen Charnock, 'is an act of the understanding applying itself to the knowledge of the excellency of God…It is also an act of the will, whereby *the soul* adores and reverences his majesty, is ravished with his amiableness, embraceth his goodness…and pitcheth all its affections upon him' (*Works*, 1.298).

Whether we are directing our praise to him, or receiving truth from God's Word, it is the mind that must be active and edified. Emotions will then respond to what is recognised in the mind.

We repeat yet again that in Christian worship we have the privilege of many beautiful tunes, and we are allowed to sing with accompaniment, but these must be kept within reasonable bounds, so that we never depend on them to engineer our feelings. The new worship, however, is all about music and song being intentionally and blatantly used to have a direct and major influence upon the emotions. John Wycliffe, the 'morning star of the Reformation', was strongly critical of the use of song to 'stir to dancing', or to arouse the feelings in worship. He warned his contemporaries in the words of Augustine – 'As oft as the song delights me more than that which is sung, so oft I confess that I sin grievously.' Music is a wonderful gift from the Lord, but it must never rival or drown worship offered in spirit and in truth.

The same point was made by John Wesley in his advice to hymn singers written in 1781:

> 'Above all sing spiritually. Have an eye to God in every word you sing. Aim at pleasing him more than yourself or any other creature. Attend strictly to the sense of what you sing, AND SEE THAT YOUR HEART IS NOT CARRIED AWAY WITH THE SOUND, but offered to God continually; so shall your singing be such as the Lord will approve of here, and reward when he cometh in the clouds of Heaven.'

Groups, bands or orchestras are bound to introduce an ecstatic dimension to praise, against the principles of New Testament worship. Catholic worship, as we have seen, is an aesthetic offering, designed also to engage and satisfy the worshipper at the level of the emotions. It bombards the senses with smells and bells, processions, chants and so on, being not about *understanding* but making an *impression* on the senses. We have gone back to this policy in much present-day evangelicalism. The tools are different, but there can be no doubt that contemporary Christian worship shares and exploits the same theatrical and earthly aims as Rome.

One of Britain's pioneers of new worship once outlined his own pilgrimage in a magazine article. He recalled how, as a young man, he wearily rose in his pew at the beginning of a service –

> '...resigned to a miserable morning, and thought to myself how dreadful it was that the hymn we were singing had so many verses. Most of the lines made no sense to me at all. Worse still, there were three more hymns like this before the meeting was finished! The whole thing was

dreadfully boring. I tried my best to inject feeling into the "worship", but it was like squeezing a shrivelled orange for the last drop of juice, only to be disappointed when nothing came.

'Worst of all, I kept thinking over what the pastor had said at the start of the service. He told us that we would spend eternity engaged in worship. I couldn't think of a more dreadful prospect. Surely that would be eternal endurance, not eternal life!'

The writer was very frank. He was not complaining that the service was unsound or poorly conducted, he was disparaging any traditional worship service. He went on to say that he discovered enjoyment in new songs and music, because these stirred his passions and allowed him liberty for the uninhibited expression of his feelings. But why could he not identify with the great hymns of the faith in the church of his youth? Why did the directing of sincere thoughts and words to God fail to touch him, and even bored him to distraction? The answer is that for him, emotions had to be worked up by external aids, uninhibited actions, and lilting rhythms and heavy percussion. It would seem that he behaved as a lover of the world rather than a lover of God. Tragically, no one told this young man what he was getting into, and its artificiality and pandering to the flesh. No one helped him – assuming he possessed real spiritual life – to love the Lord with the heart and with the mind.

We can understand how necessary the techniques of ecstatic worship are within the charismatic movement, because of the shallowness of preaching, and large numbers of people who are not genuinely converted. They need artificial, emotional stimulation to find worship enjoyable. Similarly, in some of the so-called megachurches of the USA, where the true challenge of the Gospel is left out so as not to offend those who attend, large numbers of unconverted people depend on the external emotional impact of musical-song productions. If people are brought to easy, meaningless professions, and not truly changed by the power of the Spirit, they will obviously lack spiritual appreciation, which is the basis of true worship.

Leading exponents of new worship often speak against hymns as too cerebral and complex. They say that 'meaning' obscures 'feeling'. They want mainly choruses and simple songs, because these, with their minimal truth content, do not get in the way of the music and its effect upon the emotions.

A word must be said about the extreme exploitation of ecstatic worship, which is *mystical* worship. This happens when the emotional impact of music and song is designed to give the impression of a 'direct touch' of God, or an extraordinary sense of union with him. In non-Christian mystical religions this sensation is produced by techniques such as contemplation and repetition of thoughts. In charismatic worship it is worked up by powerful musical manipulation, participants swaying with closed eyes, upturned faces and outstretched hands, yielding themselves wholly to the impact of repeated words, and music. The words of their choruses and hymns often claim a direct touch from the Lord, or a strong sense of his surrounding arms. Instead of approaching God by faith, and reflecting on his sure Truth and his wonderful work, such worshippers manufacture a 'direct' impression of God's presence.

Mystical worship represents the extreme flank of ecstatic worship, but it now has an immense following. The understanding is barely fruitful, but this hardly matters. Spirit and truth are outmoded. Artificially induced feelings are king. This is the mystical extreme now seeping into sounder churches. Here is a widely accepted definition of worship by a conservative seminary professor in the USA:

> 'Worship is an encounter in which God's glory, Word and graces are unveiled, and we respond, in songs and prayers of celebration. Worshippers seek an encounter with the glory of God, the transcendent power and numinous mystery of the divine.'

Notice the word 'encounter'. Does he mean an encounter by faith? No, he speaks of nothing other than a mystical encounter with the *glory* of God. This is astonishing mysticism. Are we reading too much into this? No, sadly, because it is also described as an encounter with the *transcendent power* of God! The language is far too powerful to describe anything other than a felt sensation of the divine. The professor's use of the words *numinous mystery* are conclusive, because *numinous* refers to the awesome presence of divinity. This theologian seriously believes that worship must be a sensed encounter with the glorious presence of God. He goes on to show how this is produced by the contents and trappings of a service.

We must take warning that the old definitions are being discarded with indifference, sometimes even contempt, and new ideas are being propounded which are totally contrary to biblical and reformational teaching. The new worship is firmly ecstatic (and also largely mystical) rather than rational and faith-reliant. Bearing in mind those who feel that an element of new worship songs may be safely adopted by 'traditionalists' – can it be right even to sip from this unbiblical, unchristian, humanly engineered, ecstatic stream?

CHAPTER 4

THREE BROKEN PRINCIPLES
III – Sacred or Profane Worship?

THE THIRD MAJOR departure from biblical principles of worship is the modern refusal to accept the great gulf between sacred and profane, so that the entertainment forms of the world are imported into the church for the praise of God. This writer, until recently, used the term 'worldly-idiom worship' to describe this, but it lacked precision. People would naturally ask, 'What exactly is worldliness?' Is a musical style (or instrument) unsuitable for worship simply because the world uses it? We do not say that, but a musical genre becomes unsuitable for spiritual use if it has been created by the world to promote an anti-God, anti-moral agenda, and that is its chief and obvious purpose. (It is also unsuitable if it employs emotion-dominating rhythms to manipulate mood and seize hypnotic control of minds.)

The word *profane* focuses the issue more clearly. To be *profane* is to treat sacred and biblical things with irreverence or disregard, so as to violate and pollute them. Is classical music worldly or profane? Not in the main. It is not generally regarded as promoting an anti-God, anti-moral message or culture. Even compositions based on pagan fables are not seen as promoting or advancing them. Are old-fashioned folk songs profane? Not usually. Many were innocently sung for generations in the primary schools of a more moral age. (Please note that this last comment is about *old* folk songs, not the new genre.)

Is the modern entertainment scene profane? Most definitely, because it is the most powerful and determined anti-God, anti-moral, anti-authority culture for centuries. It is profane because it treats moral and sacred things with utmost irreverence and disregard. It actively and militantly decries biblical morality, substituting the opposite. It blatantly and vigorously promotes an alternative society, including the worship of self and of lust as normal, reasonable and acceptable, and that is its own boasted purpose and aim.

For this reason the new worship movement is immensely wrong, and sins against God when it borrows and employs all the distinctive components of today's popular entertainment culture. Modern worship is a total artistic identification with that culture, contrary to the exhortation of *1 John 2.15-16*:

> 'Love not the world, neither the things that are in the world. If any man love the world, the love of the Father is not in him. For all that is in the world, the lust of the flesh, and the lust of the eyes, and the pride of life, is not of the Father, but is of the world.'

Modern worship equally abuses the parallel warning of *James 4.4*:

> 'Know ye not that the friendship of the world is enmity with God? whosoever therefore will be a friend of the world is the enemy of God.'

The Lord calls for submission to his standards, and he will resist, not bless, those who set themselves above his Word. This is clear from *James 4.6.*

The need to distinguish between sacred and secular, or between sacred and profane, or spiritual and worldly has always been a ruling principle for Christians. The 'culture' of the house of God must certainly be joyful, yet at the same time honour the reverent ethos of biblical worship. Until the 1960s most evangelicals believed that the church and the world represented opposing standards and life-styles and tastes, and so most of the world's popular jollities were treated as belonging to the world. Spiritual worship was sacred and special and not to be confused or mixed with, or even tainted by, the debased end of the popular entertainment spectrum, belonging to the realm of secular and profane things. All were convinced that Almighty God would be offended, and that lost sinners could not be called out of the world by a church that had adopted the values of the world. When the rebellious pop-scene of the 1960s began to flourish, virtually every serious Christian knew that to employ in worship something wedded to a culture of free sex, godlessness and drugs would be worse than inappropriate, it would be sinful.

Christians of the recent past saw that two different worlds and kingdoms stood in stark contrast to one another, the churches being the upholders of God's sovereignty and holiness, representing the Holy and the High. They therefore rejected the help of a fleshly world and its idiom, relying instead on the power of God rather than the carnal appeal of entertainment emotionalism.

As time went by, however, the pop-style songs were picked up by numerous shallow churches, youth groups, and famous international evangelists who had come to put earthly appeal before the standards of the Lord.

There are many today who have forgotten that the father of the faithful, Abraham, was called to come out of the culture of a pagan world, and live life in an altogether distinctive way for the Lord. It is also forgotten that the children of Israel in the wilderness were severely judged for wanting to go back to the foodstuffs of Egypt, even though these were not intrinsically sinful, because God had provided something special for them. From earliest times the Lord has been teaching his church to be a distinctive people.

Under the law of Moses the people were taught in many ways to distinguish between holy and unholy, and between clean and unclean, even though it meant the forbidding of many things not inherently evil, in order to teach them the law of distinction and separation. Christians have traditionally believed (as Paul said) that these things 'were written for our learning'.

Almost countless examples occur throughout the Old Testament of divine anger at any form of blending with the culture of the nations around for worship. In Nehemiah's time, a foolish and corrupt high priest gave Tobiah the Ammonite a chamber *in the Temple*. Nehemiah 'cast forth all the household stuff of Tobiah out of the chamber' and thoroughly cleansed the whole area. The same cleansing is needed today in the temple of Christian worship. God's reproof to Israel *(Ezekiel 22.26)* applies particularly to this hour:

> 'Her priests have violated my law, and have profaned mine holy things: they have put no difference between the holy and profane, neither have they shewed difference between the unclean and the clean, and have hid their eyes from my sabbaths, and I am profaned among them.'

Some glorious words at the end of Zechariah's prophecy speak figuratively of the worship of the New Testament church, and how even the bridles of the horses will bear the words, 'HOLINESS UNTO THE LORD', and the cooking pots in the house shall be as sacred as the bowls before the altar. Nothing profane will invade. Whether we consult the Old or the New Testament, purity and separation are demanded in worship. There must be a marked distinction between sacred and secular. Wherever this world's culture distinctively serves and represents fleshly living, it is to be rejected by believers.

Historic, mainstream evangelicalism has in the past taken this very seriously. The founders and builders of virtually all Bible-believing churches existing before 1960 held tenaciously to the distinction between spiritual and worldly, and those ministers and evangelists, with their elders and people, would be universally appalled at what is happening today in the places they brought to birth. Were they wrong? Were they biblically misinformed? Were they fools, or in pathetic bondage to mere tradition?

New worship advocates repeatedly wheel out the absurd claim that today's 'traditional' hymn tunes were once controversial novelties which gradually gained acceptance. New-style worship tunes, they say, will soon be an accepted part of the landscape. In other words, defenders of traditional hymns are making a foolish and petty fuss. It is also claimed that very many 'traditional' hymn tunes were originally tavern or music-hall songs. This claim is intended to obscure the fact that Christians in the past distinguished very carefully between sacred and profane. Are these claims, which we hear so often, true? The answer must be expressed bluntly, because misinformation is so dangerous with such an important subject. These claims are historical nonsense. Those who repeat them have trusted some ignorant or mischievous source which was unworthy of their respect. We would like to trace these claims to their origin, but it seems impossible. What matters is that they are entirely incorrect. They are much-retailed myths.

The jibe is heard, for example, that Luther used tavern songs and dance tunes for his hymns. His music, it is said, was heavily influenced by the secular entertainment of the time, and new-style worship is no worse. Did Luther borrow from the secular world around him? The charge is not true. Luther loved music and wanted the people to sing. He introduced congregational hymn singing in his day and he wanted hymns to have fine tunes. Before the Reformation, the Church of Rome had no congregational singing. The people just listened. They listened to the chants and other items performed by monks and special choirs.

Luther was a composer himself, and also an adapter of other works. We read in Robert Harrell's work, *Martin Luther: His Music, His Message*, that Luther wrote thirty-seven chorales, fifteen of which he composed himself, and thirteen being derived from existing Catholic church music. Four were taken from German religious folk songs. Only one out of the thirty-seven was drawn from a secular folk song. This hardly justifies the idea that Luther helped himself to secular sources. In the case of the single item drawn from a secular folk song, it is argued that the secular world had stolen that melody from the church, and Luther merely reclaimed it (having adapted and sanitised it).

Promoters of new worship love to quote Luther as saying, 'Why should the devil have all the good tunes?' What they do not tell their hearers is that Luther was talking about Catholic church music, not tavern songs. He was not interested in stealing from the world around him. If, rarely, a secular melody was used, it was very greatly changed, and what else would we expect from the Reformer who wrote –

> 'Take special care to shun perverted minds who prostitute this lovely gift of nature and of art with their erotic rantings. And be quite assured that none but the devil goads them on to defy their very nature…They purloin the gift of God and use it to worship the foe of God.'

Luther clearly believed that music was to be identified with its source and users. It was the world of those days that often stole from the church to obtain a melody line for a bawdy bar song, but not the other way round. Clearly, as we have noted, it would not be a violation of the distinction between sacred and profane for the church to borrow from relatively innocent spheres of secular music, such as the older genre of folk melody. But generally speaking hymn tunes of the past were not drawn from any musical idiom associated with aggressive opposition to God's authority and biblical morality. Luther boldly asserted that he had never used a bar song or a dance tune. People charge him with a 'crime' of which he would have been appalled. We repeat, it is a charge not substantiated by history.

In his book, *England Before and After Wesley*, J. W. Bready tells us that in the Great Awakening of the eighteenth century –

> 'The popular hymns and choruses contained no trace of ranting jingo or syncopated clamour: they bore no kinship to the uproar and fury of

modern jazz, or to the insipidity of crooning. On the contrary, this new hymnody… was expressed in music at once lyrical, dignified, soulful and sweet.'

Does evangelical worship reinvent itself every few decades by adopting new hymn and musical forms, controversial at first, but soon becoming the *status quo*? Yes, answer the glib advocates of new worship. But let any reader just visit the second-hand bookshop in town, and pick out old hymnbooks. There may be eighteenth-century books there. As you take them up and examine them, you may be surprised to see how many of the hymns are familiar to you. They formed the backbone of conservative hymnbooks for generations until this day. Those familiar with the names of hymn tunes (often printed above the hymns) will see that most of these are still the majority tunes in conventional hymnbooks. It is remarkable how stable the worship scene has been over very many years. This is because the church of Christ has long had its very own culture of hymns and hymn tunes, formed to suit reverent, intelligent, heartfelt praise, and kept well apart from the world of profanity.

It is true that several new 'streams' of emphasis have appeared from time to time in traditional hymnody – such as the affecting, subjective hymns of the late-nineteenth-century American writers. But these have practically always held the line in steering a wide berth from profane, worldly music. They have added to, but never betrayed, the principles behind evangelical hymns. It is immensely sad to see this long-maintained testimony, based firmly on biblical principles, now torn to shreds by slick and dishonest proponents of contemporary worship. Their claims and jibes are false and even scandalous, and it is a terrible shame to see people being misled by them.

A significant statement appeared in a Christian magazine article about new worship. Thinking of 'Willow Creek', a megachurch in the USA noted for its contemporary worship, the writer said – 'Only a generation that loved Woodstock could love Willow Creek.' The worship leaders and performing artistes of Willow Creek would have been very pleased to read this, for this was exactly what they set out to achieve. Their worship was designed to close the gap between the church and the world to make the one more acceptable to the other. But according to James, to make the church resemble the world is to make it the enemy of God.

Again we will ask our simple test question – why would a church wish to increase its customary, traditional instrumentation and change its style of worship? What is the aim? What will be achieved? What can guitars plus percussion accomplish? And what will be added by the inclusion of trumpet, trombone, drums, saxophone and xylophone (now so common)? The answer may come back along these lines: 'This will commend us to the present generation, drawing them in and showing them that Christianity is not fusty, but right for them, and telling them that they have nothing to fear from us.' Such a reply will show that the biblical separation of the church from the world is no longer understood and honoured. Sacred and profane may now unite, and so eliminate the offence of the Cross.

* * * * *

The three deviations described in these pages contradict crucial principles recovered in the blaze of New Testament light that shone so brightly at the time of the Reformation. Worship is to be offered in spirit and in truth, and not by works of skill or artistry. Worship is to be directed from the understanding, our joy being a response to things we sincerely appreciate, not phoney joy generated and fuelled by 'physical' means. Worship is to be kept distinct from decadent and godless worldly culture. These principles must never be dismissed or surrendered. How we worship is not an accident of history, but the application of principles. It is not a matter of culture or genera-tion, but a matter of obeying and pleasing God the Father, to whom worship is directed, God the Son in whose name it is offered, and God the Holy Spirit, who empowers it and translates it into the 'language' of Heaven.

Reverence

There is a fourth basic principle of worship which we have detached from the three just reviewed, because this fourth did not need to be entirely rediscovered at the Reformation. Despite the widespread insincerity of the priests of the Roman Church, there was generally a realisation that awe and reverence was due to Almighty God. Professing Christianity has waited until now before deciding that reverence is optional. This fourth essential is the theme of chapter 12 – 'Reverence Begins in the Place of Worship'.

CHAPTER 5

Let the Lord Define Worship

THERE ARE no physical elements or actions in New Testament worship apart from baptism and the Lord's Supper, which were ordained by the Saviour only as figures. Thus the Lord keeps to his own words – 'God is a Spirit: and they that worship him must worship him in spirit and in truth.' It should be obvious from this that we cannot worship by dancing or by any other physical action. (Dancing and hand-raising will be touched upon in later chapters.) Equally worship cannot be conveyed by melody or instruments, music being no more than a wonderful help in the singing of praise. We should never abandon or minimise words, and try to worship through music instead.

The Lord's own definition of worship is set out in remarkable detail in a vision given to John, recorded in *Revelation* chapters 4 and 5. These chapters present a view of God's rule over his Church, and also of the Church's worship. At the centre of the scene is the glorious throne of God, with all three Persons of the Trinity present there *(Revelation 4.2 and 5; 5.1 and 6)*. Exalted language is used to describe the throne, which projects powerful phenomena symbolising the attributes of God.

Around the throne appear four 'beasts' or living creatures, usually identified as God's cherubim of justice protecting the holiness of God *(Revelation 4.6-9)*. Also, before the throne is a great sea of glass, probably representing the atoning merits and the offered-up righteousness of Jesus Christ, the only means of approaching the throne *(Revelation 4.6)*.

Outside and around that sea of glass, often pictured as forming a vast circle, are twenty-four elders, representing twelve patriarchs and twelve apostles, in other words, all believers (of both Testaments). This is the Church, both Jew and Gentile, past, present and future; the entire company of redeemed people *(Revelation 4.4 and 10)*. Outside and around that circle stands the angelic host, numbering ten thousand times ten thousand, and thousands of thousands.

In the course of this vision we discover how God's people, both in Heaven and upon earth, worship God. In *Revelation 4.8* we read of how the cherubim of justice, perhaps the very highest angels, express praise. 'And the four beasts had each of them six wings about him; and they were full of eyes within: and they rest not day and night, SAYING, Holy, holy, holy, Lord God Almighty.' The word of tremendous significance to notice is that single word – 'saying'. They *said* their worship. (It was an audible statement whether said or sung.)

Then, in verses 10 and 11 we read of how the Church of all ages worships. 'The four and twenty elders fall down before him... and cast their crowns before the throne, SAYING, Thou art worthy, O Lord.' They also *spoke* (or sang) their worship. They used words.

In chapter 5.8-9 we read: 'And when he had taken the book, the four beasts and four and twenty elders fell down before the Lamb, having every one of them harps, and golden vials full of odours, which are the prayers of saints. And they SUNG a new song.' They *sang* words of worship.

In verses 11 and 12 we are told how the main company of angels worship. 'And I beheld, and I heard the voice of many angels round about the throne and the beasts and the elders: and the number of them was ten thousand times ten thousand, and thousands of thousands; SAYING with a loud voice, Worthy is the Lamb.' They *spoke* forth (or sang) their magnificent statement of adoration.

In verse 13, the record says that every person and every angel will acknowledge that God is over all, and they will do so in intelligent words. 'And every creature which is in heaven, and on the earth, and under the earth, and such as are in the sea, and all that are in them, heard I SAYING, Blessing, and honour, and glory, and power, be unto him that sitteth upon the throne.' In the very next verse we are told once again that 'the four beasts SAID'. This is the worship of God in both Heaven and earth. They all *said* or *sang*.

In this vision of true worship, we see only one form of worship – and that is *words*. We must affirm this most emphatically – in God's own definition worship takes the form of *words*. Worship is not words *and* music. Music certainly assists, but the valid part is the words, whether thought, said or sung. There is no other vehicle of worship aside from words. The rational mind is the seat of worship. Of course, worship is by faith and love, but it has to be in words, and this fact is a central standard of historic biblical Christianity. This is why the Reformation cast aside all Roman Catholic theatricalism.

When we say that the Bible defines worship as something expressible in intelligible words, a query arises about praying with 'groanings which cannot be uttered', mentioned by Paul in *Romans 8*. Is this not prayer without words? The answer is, no, for the simple reason that these groanings are not ours, but those of the Holy Spirit. With our thoughts we pray in words, and the Holy Spirit sifts them, translates them into the language of Heaven, and conveys them with divine feeling to the eternal throne on our behalf. We do not know what to pray for, or how to pray as we ought, but the Holy Spirit takes our stumbling efforts, beautifies and perfects them, and presents them before the Father.

We should never say, therefore, 'I may pray just by feeling, even though I cannot express it in words.' It may happen that a believer feels so strongly about something that his feelings seem to outpace his mind, but if asked, he should be able to say what he prayed for. There is no prayer that cannot be put into words. We must pray, says Paul, with the understanding. Every genuine prayer passes through the rational mind, and this alone is true worship. Anything other than this is mystical worship, the essence of occult religion, and is not biblical Christianity.

It is a matter of fact that if this chapter had been written 100 years ago, most Bible-believing readers would have thought it too obvious to be printed. They all knew this. It was fundamental to them that *worship is words.* In recent times, tragically, this principle has been widely forgotten, and fundamentals have slipped out of sight. Very strong feelings may be experienced in our worship, but these should always arise from and support the coherent thoughts of our mind. We must feel things because we think them. If we truly understand and mean the words, then the Holy Spirit (who inspires all genuine worship) will touch our minds so that we see these things even more clearly, and he will also touch our hearts so that we *feel* what we see all the more strongly. The emotional system is a system of support and response, and not the prime mover in worship. It should never be stirred into action or 'worked up' by musical techniques.

In his pastoral epistles, the apostle Paul makes many exhortations about sound-mindedness. He calls for rational control at all times, insisting on sensible words and thoughts. He insists that the rational faculty must always be switched on. By these exhortations he condemns purely sentimental worship (and trances also). In *1 Corinthians* he tells us that we pray and sing in the spirit, but always with the understanding also.

Guided by the Lord's own definition and picture of true worship, we do not major on instrumental excitement and pleasure, but meaningful word-content in hymns, prayers, and preaching. Here will be the deep things of God, and distinctive reverence, power and glory.

Is traditional worship too cerebral?

One well-known writer critiquing modern worship rightly charged its promoters with 'dumbing down' worship. The promoters claim that traditional worship is too cerebral, and its defenders are held captive by matters of 'taste'. Theologian John Frame says the trouble with defenders of traditional worship is that they are musical and theological snobs. But it is not snobbery to be alarmed at the new worship. John Frame tells us he is delighted with choruses and other short, repetitive songs simply because there are very few thoughts in them. For him this is a virtue. He takes a verse from a hymn of Wesley and pronounces it inferior to a conspicuously vapid chorus as a means of efficient communication. His problem with Wesley and Watts and every other traditional hymnwriter is that they say far too much. No one, apparently, can grasp all their thoughts, for they are too numerous and too sophisticated. Millions of believers over the centuries have (in Frame's opinion) been left behind by over-complex worship.

Frame attempts some curious interpretations of Scripture to justify his denigration of great hymns. He looks at Job, noting the fine speeches he prepared to hurl at God when the opportunity arose. But when Job heard God's voice, he put his hand over his mouth, and choked out the simplest words. Says Frame – that is the right way. That is the difference between traditional worship and new worship. *Traditional* is like Job's fine speeches, and *contemporary worship* is evidently what Job should have done all along. It all proves that the fewest words and the strongest feelings are best. Moses and Isaiah are also brought into the argument by John Frame. They fell silent before the Lord, and said very little. This fact apparently supports the shortage of meaningful words in contemporary Christian worship. Such arguments will strike most readers as being irrelevant and even absurd, but we have not yet seen an advocate of new worship who can offer anything more credible. They simply cannot find scriptural support for the downgrading of words.

Writers like John Frame say repeatedly that we must be biblical in these matters, but they never refer to the Lord's own hymnbook – the *Psalms* – in deciding what hymns should be like. It is a fact that the 'mathematics' of the *Psalms* are quite closely represented in most traditional evangelical hymnbooks. The complexity factor is similar, the ratio of praise to petition is strikingly close, and the same range of topics is accommodated. This is surprising, as it is unlikely that all editors sought a conscious correlation. It surely indicates the natural psalm-like balance of traditional reformed worship. (See charts on pages 83-84.) However, the song books of the new worship scene in no way reflect the balance of the *Psalms*. New worship songs almost cry out against the balance and structure of the *Psalms*. It is worth noting, for example, that the modern chorus has no equivalent in the *Psalms*, as our table at the end of this chapter shows. We value choruses for children, but should they be found in adult worship, when the Lord never inspired any? Are our traditional hymns too complex? When God compiled a hymnbook for an agricultural people (who were probably 95% illiterate), he gave them not a book of choruses, but the book of *Psalms*. (We are not, of course, objecting to choruses that appear as refrains at the end of hymn verses, but to the substituting of hymns with choruses.)

There is a world of difference between 'traditional' worship and new worship at this point. If we bring short choruses with oft-repeated lines and shallow sentiments into adult worship, we severely strain the Lord's demand for meaningful understanding of profound and glorious truths.

From the Psalter all the way down to the Reformation, and through subsequent centuries, great hymns (contrary to what is claimed by new-worship promoters) have been clearly understood and appreciated by the Lord's people. Indeed, hymns have lifted up

Christians not only spiritually but even intellectually. The Bible first, and godly hymns second, have taught the great truths of the Word, liberating generations from ignorance and naivety, and articulating intelligent praise. Today, the new worship is pulling believers down to an intellectual and spiritual level lower than ever before in church history.

Our point throughout this chapter is that the only vehicle of worship is intelligible thoughts and words. Contemporary or new worship discards this central fact, minimising the role of the mind and emphasising the artificial stimulation of feelings.

The Psalter is Nothing Like a Book of Choruses

All psalms (except five) contain sufficient matter to be converted into paraphrases or hymns of at least five hymn stanzas in short or common metre. Most psalms are *much* longer than this. Only the following psalms (3%) have fewer than five verses, and these cannot be regarded as choruses for the following reasons:

> *Psalm 117* (2 verses). Obviously a closing doxology, either for singing at the end of other psalms or the Temple services.

> *Psalm 123* (4 verses). This is still too long for a chorus, with too much matter. Lyte's 'Unto thee I lift my eyes' tracks this psalm in four verses.

> *Psalm 131* (3 verses). A very personal psalm to be uttered in great humility. Designed to be sung annually by pilgrims going up to Jerusalem, it is nothing like a modern chorus.

> *Psalm 133* (3 verses). Another annual pilgrimage song, this has the character of a 'grace' for meals, or for times when relations gather in reunion.

> *Psalm 134* (3 verses). Last of the pilgrim songs, this is an antiphonal blessing. In verses 1-2 the people bless the priests and Levites, and in verse 3 the latter reply.

The refrain of *Psalm 136*

Each verse of *Psalm 136* (26 verses) includes the refrain, 'For his mercy endureth for ever'. This is not a chorus, because each time it occurs it accompanies a line making a fresh, substantial point. A similar refrain is found in the first four verses of *Psalm 118*. Nowhere else does this occur in the Psalter.

CHAPTER 6

Brass, Strings and Percussion?

The facts about Bible instruments and their use

WHAT DOES the Bible teach about how instruments should be used in worship? Those who endorse the use of solo instrumental 'numbers', and bands or groups, point to the Old Testament and say that God allowed all kinds of instruments and large orchestras to contribute a major musical element to worship. If God, they reason, is the same yesterday, today and for ever, he must want a similar kind of worship today.

But is it true that God allowed full instrumental worship in the Jewish church? Is it true that the Israelites regularly worshipped with percussion instruments and brass, generating powerful, rhythmic music? Is it true that timbrels (tambourines), played by dancing maidens, led the worship? A brief look at the biblical facts will show that these ideas are sheer fiction. The very opposite is the case, for in the Old Testament era God put very firm restrictions on the use of instruments, obviously to prevent the over-enjoyment of music at the *human* level overpowering *spiritual* worship. Certainly, instruments were allowed, but only some, and only at specified times. The Old Testament lays down rules of restraint which are thrown away by new-style worshippers.

A well-known preacher said that if *Psalm 150* is full of instruments, then we can also use them today, but in saying this he was obviously unaware that several of the instruments named were either banned from the house of God, or used in a very restricted role. They are named in *Psalm 150* as a figure or picture only, but not used literally, as we shall show later in this chapter. That preacher, although he believed the Bible to be inerrant, made it contradict itself because he was ignorant of the rules (laid down in *1 Chronicles*). Here we will set out the facts about worship in the Old Testament.

We realise that the church of Jesus Christ is not under the rules of the Old Testament, and their regulations for worship do not bind us today. However, the *general principles* of caution in the use of instruments taught then by God still apply. This is why we must expose the wild and inaccurate claim that God prescribed extensive instrumental and rhythmic worship.

Before looking at the facts, one general point must be made. The promoters of new-style worship say that we may do almost anything in worship, so long as it is done to the glory of God. Any instrument or style of music we play (they say) in our private or social life, we may also use to the glory of God in worship. That is the reasoning put forward by the advocates of contemporary worship. This policy, however, is wrong because it overlooks one of the most fundamental facts of worship taught throughout the Bible, that God distinguishes *direct worship* from all other things done by his children. All that we do in life must be done to his glory, but *direct worship* is a uniquely special activity, governed by God's own rules and guidelines. By the time of King David the Israelites were using a wide range of musical instruments in their social life, but only some were allowed in direct worship, for this was a distinctive activity. We shall see that the Old Testament speaks of at least eight kinds of instrument that were in common use by the people of those days in their private and civic life, but only four of these were permitted in the house of God. It is highly important to be aware of this. We will look first at some of the excluded instruments (the texts appear later).

One 'banned' instrument was the flute. We read of various items in the flute family such as the ordinary flute, also the pipe (a flute, usually double, played sideways) with three to four holes, and the 'dulcimer' *(KJV)* – a double flute from Greece with bellows attached.* But no kind of flute was allowed in Temple worship.[1] Why was this? Because the Lord was teaching that some restrictions were necessary, so that people would not be distracted from sincere worship by too many interesting and beautiful things.

Other instruments used by the Jews but excluded from the Temple were the timbrel or tabret, which was a tambourine, and the 'organ', which was a seven-to-ten-pipe giant mouth organ (probably with reeds). All these could be used for recreation and outdoor civic festivals, but not in the house of God. The modern claim, therefore, that anything could be used, is made in ignorance of the facts. The rules were very firm, and while we are not under those rules today, it is wrong to claim that the Old Testament justifies what is happening in worship today.

Where does this information about restrictions come from? It is plainly set out in the Bible. In various texts *(1 Chronicles 15.16, 28; 16.5, 6, 42; 25.1, 6)* we read of the instruments appointed in the time of David, by divine inspiration, to be used in direct worship in the Tabernacle and Temple. We will see shortly that these limited instruments were cut even further for 'local' and private worship. The Temple instruments were psaltery, harp and cymbals,[2] which were to be played by Levites. Only the priests were to employ the trumpet (including the cornet) for special purposes,[3] but not for the normal

---

*   This translation is *KJV* only. A real dulcimer is a stringed instrument.

1, 2, 3   See Appendix notes 1 to 3, page 99, for more on biblical musical instruments.

accompaniment of singing. We repeat, these four were only half the number of instruments in common social use at the time.

At the time of King Hezekiah these rules were reaffirmed in *2 Chronicles 29.25-29*:

> 'He set the Levites in the house of the Lord with cymbals, with psalteries, and with harps, according to the commandment of David, and of Gad the king's seer . . . for so was the commandment of the Lord by his prophets. And the Levites stood with the instruments of David, and the priests with the trumpets.'

The trumpets had only a limited role:

> 'And when the burnt offering began, the song of the Lord began also with the trumpets, and with the instruments ordained by David king of Israel. And all the congregation worshipped, and the singers sang, and the trumpeters sounded: and all this continued until the burnt offering was finished. And when they had made an end of offering, the king and all that were present with him bowed themselves, and worshipped.'

The trumpets called the people to solemn assemblies and accompanied the burning of the offering. This was a serious, awe-producing, and even shame-producing activity. The Hebrew term for 'solemnity' appears in the description of these acts of worship, and it is therefore obvious that the trumpets were sounded so as to stir people to reverence and gravity, and that the cymbals (to hold the timing of the singing) were played soberly.

Of course, the worship had a strongly joyful element arising from the great themes sung, but we note that there were no drums or tambourines in the orchestra (as there are today on very many church platforms). We also note that the instruments were only played during the burning of the offering, and then the music ended, and everyone continued to worship without them.

At the time of David the orchestra of the house of the Lord appears to have consisted of twenty-seven Levite musicians playing just three types of instrument *(1 Chronicles 25.1-6)*.[4] This was an

---

4   See Appendix note 4 about Heman's horn.

extremely modest orchestra to carry the singing of several thousand worshippers.[5] From this rather small provision, it is clear that this music was not designed to dominate (or detract from) intelligent, feelingful worship.

Centuries later, when Temple worship was restored by Ezra and Nehemiah, the four-instrument rule was scrupulously followed, confirming that it was a binding rule for the Jews. (See *Ezra 3.10* and *Nehemiah 12.27*.)

All these instructions applied firstly to the *second stage* of the recovery of the ark,[2] and later to all worship in the Temple. The same instrumentation, however, was not prescribed for local synagogue worship.[6] This was much simpler, the cymbals and trumpets disappearing, making it even more impossible to read a big-beat idea into the Bible. The stringed instruments appointed for worship were sweet rather than clamourous. In the book of *Psalms* we see that harps and psalteries were the only intended instruments for the accompaniment of worship in private or synagogue worship, there being no brass or percussion. The very title 'Psalter' is by definition a collection of songs sung to harp accompaniment. *Psalm 92* provides an example of this instruction, the title or heading over the psalm saying that it was 'A Psalm or Song for the sabbath day', and the third verse saying it should be sung to an instrument of ten strings, the psaltery and harp with a solemn sound. The following psalms also state clearly the rule that psalms were to be sung to harps and psalteries: *Psalms 33, 43, 57, 71, 92, 108, 144* and *147*. In *Psalms 4, 6, 54, 55, 61, 67* and *76* the inscription (at the top of the psalm) prescribes stringed instruments ('Neginoth'). In *Psalm 12* the title probably prescribes an eight-stringed lyre (a type of harp). It was with such modest and sweet-sounding instruments that singing was supported in domestic and synagogue worship.[7]

2, 5, 6, 7   See Appendix notes 2, 5 and 6, and note 7 for more information on inscriptions.

Does the Bible contradict itself?

The rules of the Old Testament are clear, but they sometimes seem to be contradicted in the *Psalms*. Advocates of new-style worship point to passages such as *Psalm 68.25* where David mentions 'the damsels playing with timbrels', and claim that this justifies the use of a tambourine. In three other psalms also David seems to contradict his own rules (or rather, those that God gave him). The Bible, however, has no contradictions. It is not possible that God would give definite commands in one place, and totally contradict them in another, and this should make us examine more carefully those passages which *seem* to contradict the rules. When we do so, we see at once that the banned instruments were not being used in the direct worship of God, but in civic, outdoor festivals held to commemorate great battle victories of the past.

We should never forget that the Israelites were a *nation state* as well as a *church*. There were many things they were permitted to do as a state, which had no place in their formal, direct worship. Special processions, victory parades and thanksgiving days were open-air, civic activities organised by God's people in their capacity as a *state*. The little girls would lead open-air processions, dancing and shaking their tambourines, but these tambourines were never allowed in the house of God. A direct act of worship was quite different from a civic anniversary celebration.

The timbrel-tambourine of *Psalm 68* is obviously part of a civic activity. The psalm, though predictive and Messianic, is based on a notable military victory. It refers to the chariots of God, and how a conqueror led a host of captives after a mighty battle. God's power is remembered not only in the sanctuary but also in street festivities, during which 'the singers went before, the players on instruments followed after; among them were the damsels playing with timbrels.' The psalm certainly includes reference to direct worship, but it mentions timbrels in connection with open-air national 'remembrance', and there is no contradiction of the Temple rules.

In *Psalm 81.2* the timbrel is found again. 'Take a psalm, and bring hither the timbrel, the pleasant harp with the psaltery.' It is a psalm of Asaph. Was he breaking the rules and including a prohibited instrument in worship? The answer is no, for his psalm is a summons to the people to join in the worship and festivities of the Feast of Tabernacles, commemorating the deliverance of the people from Egypt, their survival in the wilderness, and the 'harvest' of the Promised Land. During the seven days of the feast all Israelites lived in 'booths' or 'tents' made of palm branches symbolising the tents of the wilderness journeyings. This feast, with its offerings, was also the nation's annual harvest festival. It was obviously a time when virtually every outdoor cultural instinct was given expression, and much music accompanied the long processions of Israelites journeying to Jerusalem for the feast. Naturally, the 'maidens' played their timbrels, and the Hebrew national dance was probably in evidence during the evening hours in every camp.

With these scenes of national festivity in mind we realise that Asaph made no mistake over the instruments. He did not add the tambourine to the Temple orchestra, nor prescribe it as an instrument for direct worship.

Psalm 98.5-6 mentions the harp for accompanying psalm singing, and adds trumpets. These were to be blown by the priests on special feast days only. Sure enough, this psalm includes the commemoration of great victories, and the worship of special days is therefore in mind. The formula is as ever – tambourines and cultural dance were permitted for national festivities, sweet, harp-like instruments for personal and local, normal worship, and solemn trumpets (played by priests) and cymbals (played only by choir leaders such as Asaph) added for Temple worship.

As we have seen, *Psalms 149-150* are constantly quoted by the promoters of new-style worship as a justification for the uninhibited use of instruments (along with dancing) in direct worship. *Psalm*

149 includes the verse, 'Let them praise his name in the dance: let them sing praises unto him with the timbrel and harp' (verse 3). The question is – Does the psalmist refer to direct worship, or to the national festivities of the Jews, including the victory festivals with all their outdoor rejoicing? As we read through the psalm the answer becomes obvious. *Psalm 149* is not exclusively about direct worship, for it ranges widely over every aspect of national and private life. This wide-ranging scope of the psalm is obvious from the fifth verse, which encourages the people to sing aloud upon their beds. The sixth verse exhorts them to praise God with a two-edged sword in their hands. Were they literally to take beds and swords into the Temple, and somehow employ them in direct worship? Obviously not. The scope of the psalm includes private worship during the night, and also military service for the land. The seventh verse of the psalm calls for vengeance to be executed upon the heathen, and the eighth for their kings to be bound with chains. This would never have happened in the house of God. It is obviously referring to a victory pageant in Israel's national life. It therefore covers every aspect of life, both civic and spiritual. This includes civic festivities and victory pageants, and so we should not be surprised to find tambourines and dancing referred to. The rules for Temple worship are not contradicted.

What about *Psalm 150*? The psalmist summons God's people to praise him with tambourines, dance, and organs alongside the permitted Temple instruments. (The organ, we have already observed, was a wind instrument of between seven and ten pipes.) The psalm opens – 'Praise ye the Lord. Praise God in his sanctuary: praise him in the firmament of his power.' The 'sanctuary' mentioned here is described as God's 'mighty expanse' or 'mighty heavens'.[8] It is not the earthly Temple, but the temple of the entire universe, even of the infinite expanse beyond the universe where angels fly at God's

---

8   See Appendix note 8.

command. In other words, this is another psalm calling for God to be glorified in every department of life. It goes beyond direct acts of worship. The sixth verse of the psalm reminds us that instruments cannot themselves be a channel of praise. Only things that have breath can worship. Only living souls can praise the Lord. In the light of this, the psalm only makes sense when understood as a richly figurative psalm, using the tone characteristics of various instruments to describe the different emotions of true worship.

Puritan David Dickson expressed this in his renowned commentary on the *Psalms*. He observed that:

'the plurality and variety of these instruments were fit to represent divers conditions of the spiritual man ... and to teach what stirring up there should be of the affections and powers of our soul for God's worship. What melody each should make in himself ... to show the excellence of God's praise, which no instrument, nor any expression of the body could sufficiently set forth with trumpet, psaltery, etc.'

The nineteenth-century Scottish preacher Andrew Bonar wrote:

'In this psalm's enumeration of musical instruments, there is a reference to the variety which exists among men in the mode of expressing joy, and in the mode of exciting feeling.'

The psalm, in other words, lists the instruments not as those to be literally used in the house of God, but as representing the range of themes or attitudes which make up heartfelt worship. By this interpretation the instruments are figurative and representative. This is the most common interpretation of this psalm by commentators of the reformed tradition. The *trumpet* (verse 3) represents the note of victory. The *psaltery* and the *harp* give the sweet tones of gratitude and love. The *timbrel* and the *dance* (verse 4) speak of the effervescent energy, effort and enthusiasm of children engaged in a favourite activity. Accordingly, worship demands energy of mind, and enthusiasm of soul from believers. *Organs* were instruments of pleasure rather than worship, and we are therefore reminded that true praise should be the highest enjoyment of believers, not merely a mechanical duty. The fifth verse brings in loud and resounding *cymbals*, a probable allusion to the volume, strength and power of worthy praise, but doubtless also an allusion to the deeply awe-inspiring humbling of true worship.

A recently published, popular Study Bible remarks that this psalm calls for praise with all kinds of musical instruments, but to take this very literal view of the psalm is absurd, producing a major contradiction in the Bible. God is seen to make firm rules, and then to call for them to be broken. *Psalm 150* cannot and does not cancel the limitations on Old Testament instruments of worship.

Someone may object that the church organ of today is a large number of instruments bound together in one. In a sense, this is so, but it is played by a single instrumentalist, a rather obvious restriction on its versatility. Because its voices are united into one general sound, it may be regarded (when played reasonably and sensibly) as a single instrument.

The standard of God remains in this Gospel age – that musical instruments should be modest in character, limited in number, and never allowed to rival or overwhelm the attractiveness of intelligent worship. The idea that the Old Testament sanctions the musical antics of the present time is based on an amazingly superficial and mistaken view of the biblical data. Worship was never supposed to be an opportunity for human exhibitionism.

A constantly recurring theme of Scripture is that God resists the proud. Worship is not to show off human artistic ability, nor to entertain worshippers. Music and instrumental expertise must never be allowed to interfere with the spiritual character of worship. Traditional worship promotes awe, reverence, spirituality and thoughtfulness. Joy flows from the meaning of the sentiments, and is not worked up by the use of external helps. Traditional worship is based on biblical worship, which avoids earthly musical distractions. The Lord trusts his people to use musical helps to assist their praise, but that trust must never be abused. Yet today, we contend, this trust is being abused by the advocates of modern-style worship.

CHAPTER 7

Services of Worship in the Bible

IS THERE AN EXAMPLE of a worship service in the Bible? There is, virtually, because several portions of Scripture provide illuminating snapshots of worship. *Revelation* chapters 4 and 5, referred to already, provide key insights into the arrangement, tone and matter of praise. Worship, in this passage, begins with a view of the four living creatures around the throne, saying, 'Holy, holy, holy, Lord God Almighty, which was, and is, and is to come.' It is highly important to note that objective praise comes first. God is named and described by several of the divine attributes – his holiness, sovereignty, power and eternity. Worshippers give glory and honour and thanks to the eternal Ruler, the entire initial focus being upon him, subjective thanksgiving being left till later.

The next contribution to worship noted in this great passage is by the four and twenty elders (representing the Church of all ages) who fall down in humility and worship the eternal God. They also begin with objective praise, casting their crowns before the throne, acknowledging God as their sovereign ruler and source of salvation, and saying, 'Thou art worthy, O Lord, to receive glory and honour and power: for thou hast created all things, and for thy pleasure they are and were created' *(Revelation 4.11)*. God alone is in their view, and he is adored and extolled. His sovereign will is mentioned ('for thy pleasure'), and he is acknowledged as exclusively deserving worship. The minds of the worshippers are focused entirely upon him, and his qualities.

Our worship services must surely reflect this order. We too should begin worship with objective praise expressed in grand and worthy terms. This is the great spiritual tradition of Reformation worship, although many have lost touch with these basic principles today, and services frequently begin with lyrics of subjective testimony.

The next contribution appears in *Revelation 5.9-10*, where the living creatures and the twenty-four elders join in singing about God's plan for the ages (represented by the book with seven seals). They sing of Christ, his worthiness and his atoning death for people of every tribe and nation. At this point subjective thanksgiving appears, as they sing of Christ having 'redeemed *us*'. Then they speak more specifically of themselves, their song being one of amazement, gratitude, and rejoicing. They sing of how Christ has 'made us unto our God kings and priests: and we shall reign on the earth'. They sing about their wonderful status as God's children, of the priesthood of all believers, and of their coming eternal reign with Christ. In other words, they mingle their thanksgiving with the reviewing of solid truths.

The next contribution is made by the vast, countless host of angels, who say with a loud voice, 'Worthy is the Lamb that was slain to receive power, and riches, and wisdom, and strength, and honour, and glory, and blessing' *(Revelation 5.12)*. In this magnificent burst of objective praise, God's infinite glory and attributes are ascribed to the Lord Jesus Christ. On hearing these words, the four living creatures and the twenty-four elders fall down and worship, their falling down showing their humble submission and dedication to him

– these being essential attitudes of heart in worship. Is this not the opposite of what we see on the platform in modern services, where musical artistes soak up praise and applause?

We summarise that biblical worship is firstly *objective*, being about God, and his wonderful works. Only secondly is it about us, and what he has done for us. There is also the review of great truths, along with submission and commitment. The keynote is undoubtedly reverence and humility, the language being lofty and entirely scriptural. We see no familiarity of the kind that brings God down to the level of human relationships (the kind of praying and singing we hear so often nowadays). God remains throughout the revered, everlasting Father, and the eternal King-Saviour. We note that while the words are profound, the format is unadorned. Worshippers bring no offering of substance or skill. They bring only words, offered from their hearts, but these are words taught them by God.

Not all the elements of worship are represented in this *Revelation* passage. There is no repentance, for example, or intercession, for the location of worship is in Heaven. Nevertheless, the scene is almost complete as an example of a service of worship.

Another snapshot of biblical worship is to be seen in *Acts 4.24-30*, where the apostles and others after hearing Peter and John report on their arrest and release, pray for help and blessing.

'And when they heard that, they lifted up their voice to God with one accord, and said, Lord, thou art God, which hast made heaven, and earth, and the sea, and all that in them is: who by the mouth of thy servant David hast said, Why did the heathen rage, and the people imagine vain things? The kings of the earth stood up, and the rulers were gathered together against the Lord, and against his Christ. For of a truth against thy holy child Jesus, whom thou hast anointed, both Herod, and Pontius Pilate, with the Gentiles, and the people of Israel, were gathered together, for to do whatsoever thy hand and thy counsel determined before to be done. And now, Lord, behold their threatenings: and grant unto thy servants, that with all boldness they may speak thy word, by stretching forth thine hand to heal; and that signs and wonders may be done by the name of thy holy child Jesus.'

The prayer begins by naming the Lord as Maker of all things. It proceeds to quote Scripture in predicting the situation in which they found themselves. After this the Saviourhood of Christ is affirmed, and the eternal plan of God in the Gospel. Only then do they ask for blessing upon their ministry, and for the promised signs to accompany them.

Summarising the picture of worship in *Revelation 4-5,* we emphasise several features which are clearly directive for Christian churches. The worship is simple and unadorned, not an occasion for the exhibition of musical skills or individual talents. The elders had harps, simple stringed instruments, but these are actually symbolic as they are mentioned in the same breath as 'golden vials full of odours' (the prayers of saints). The *format* of worship must obviously be word-based, not majoring on music, if it is to truly glorify God.

In applying these things for ourselves today, it follows that word-based worship is bound to be somewhat predictable, judged by the flesh. Promoters of contemporary worship have complained about the 'hymn-prayer sandwich' followed in traditional worship, claiming it is dull and samish. But simplicity and predictability disappear when the words are truly appreciated and meant. It is of great value that worshippers do not sit in the pews wondering what will come next, a novelty perhaps, or a stunning item of entertainment masquerading as worship. We set out below all the biblical components of worship, each one being vital, precious and profoundly enjoyable in a right sense to sincere worshippers.

Constant interjections and interruptions by the person leading worship, however well intended, should be restrained. Often these are light and insubstantial comments made in the interests of informality, but they plainly war against the grandness and glory of the kind of worship seen in *Revelation 4-5*. Even well-motivated interjections such as introductory explanations of hymns may disrupt the focus of the congregation if they are longer than a sentence or two. Earnest humility is the best way for those who lead in worship, the motto of John the Baptist being their rule – 'He must increase, but I must decrease.'

The components of worship

If we set out in order the elements or parts of worship in the passages just considered and combine them with the elements observed in the *Psalms* and also in New Testament prayers, we arrive at the listings below. These set out the broad themes of worship which have been advocated for generations in biblical churches. Preaching is, of course, a vital and prominent feature of worship, but for this study we are considering only the non-preaching elements. (Our forebears clearly thought very deeply about these matters.)

Objective worship

1. Calling upon God (invocation) – naming God's titles, expressing our desire to approach and worship, expressing humility, and asking for help in worship.

2. Worship – adoration, praise, and blessing, focusing on the attributes of God, and the person and redemptive work of the Lord Jesus Christ.

3. Thanksgiving – for salvation in general; for personal salvation; for the Word of God; for spiritual protection and keeping; for temporal blessings.

4. Affirmation – including trust, the admiration of great doctrines of the faith, coupled with profession of faith in these things.

Subjective worship

5. Repentance – sincerely confessing and renouncing sins of commission and omission.

6. Desire for holiness – without which repentance is hollow. Here we make promises and pledges to avoid sin, and seek the help of God in giving us lively consciences, and in achieving godly behaviour.

7. Dedication and surrender – the fresh and emphatic commitment of believers' lives to obedience and the service of the Lord in the week ahead, including witness.

8. Intercession – for the lost, for the land, for the Lord's people, for

the sick and the sad, for those with great trials, for the Lord's servants, and for the persecuted.

9. Pleading (ie: petitions) – prayers of asking in which the
petitioners' specific needs are presented. This department of worship
includes the naming of God's promises, with trust and thanksgiving;
as we thank God for them we comfort our souls, and feed on them.
Specific needs will include deliverance from trials, help, strength,
illumination for understanding the Word, guidance, love for God,
boldness and instrumentality. Generally speaking we should put
spiritual needs first and temporal needs second.

Isaac Watts encapsulated most of these elements of worship in
a brilliant verse composed for his classic work, *A Guide to Prayer*
(1715):

> *Call upon God, adore, confess,*
> *Petition, plead, and then declare*
> *You are the Lord's, give thanks, and bless,*
> *And let Amen confirm the prayer.*

The order of a service

Coming to details, a typical service would traditionally open
either with an 'introit' of Scripture sentences, or with a brief prayer
calling upon God, giving glory to him, extolling his majesty and
sovereignty, acknowledging dependence upon Christ and Calvary,
and also on the Holy Spirit, and asking for forgiveness, and blessing
in worship. (Episcopalians, Methodists and Presbyterians histori-
cally preferred the former, while Baptists, Independents, Brethren
and old-style Pentecostalists preferred the latter.)

The first hymn in a service should be about God – an objective
affirmation of his attributes and glory, combining awe, gladness, and
fervour. In this we follow the pattern of the Lord's Prayer: 'After this
manner therefore pray ye: Our Father which art in heaven, Hallowed
be thy name.' After prayer and the singing of a hymn, comes the first
reading of God's Word. (There should ideally be two readings of
Scripture in a service.) A simple but widely used order would be as
follows:

Opening prayer

First hymn
(objective)

First reading of the Word
(a psalm or an Old Testament portion)

Second hymn

Second reading of the Word

Notices and offertory
(a controversial matter)

Pastoral prayer

Third hymn

Preaching of the Word
(perhaps closing in prayer)

Fourth hymn

Closing prayer

What is to be done with the notices? Some feel that because notices interrupt the worship, a word of welcome with announcements should be given *before* the worship begins. Others feel that this impedes quiet and reverent preparation for worship, possibly also blunting the objective praise which immediately follows. Still others have placed notices at the end of the service, which also has the obvious disadvantage of interfering with the heart-response to the preaching of the Word. This writer takes the view that notices may reasonably be set within the service as long as they do not contain trivial, domestic announcements or homely, 'cheerful-chappie' remarks by the person who gives them.

The main pastoral prayer in a service should be fairly predictable in its general order, although the one praying should think out fresh themes and constructions within that order. The best way is to follow the order of the departments of worship listed earlier, and to include reference to them all. The importance of full-orbed worship, with reverence and awe, and also with joy and gratitude, cannot be over-emphasised. If we are to wean believers from music-based, emotionally 'worked-up' worship, then our public praying must be along lines that will grip the mind and lift the soul in addressing intelligent words to God. The pastoral prayer (the so-called 'long prayer') in a main Sunday teaching service will be fairly substantial, whereas the pastoral prayer in an evangelistic preaching service will ideally be much shorter, and largely focused on salvation themes.

Public prayer should always be offered in the name of Jesus Christ, in obedience to his repeated command.* Ministers often enrich the Christian formula with additional reverent adjectives. It is insufficient and disrespectful toward the Saviour simply to say, 'In thy Son's name', even worse to say, 'In thy name', when prayer is addressed to the Father, as it should be.

While speaking of the titles of the Lord, it is worth noting that his familiar name – Jesus – is excessively used alone nowadays during public prayer. However, the Lord should always be referred to reverently as the Lord Jesus Christ, or at least the Lord Jesus, or by his office of Saviour. (It may be protested that the prayer of *Acts 4* uses only the name 'Jesus', but this is not so, because the Lord's divinity is stated in the words, 'by the name of thy holy child Jesus'.)

Helps for the promotion of reverence

We put forward here a few practical remarks on reverence, although the absolute necessity of reverence will be addressed in chapter 12 of this book. Reverence as well as rejoicing is a first principle of worship, and must be safeguarded in the very *setting* of the service as well as in its content. A congregation should keep silence

---

* *John 14.13-14; 15.16; 16.23 and 26. See also Ephesians 5.20; Colossians 3.17; 1 Peter 2.5.*

before the service begins, so that all may prepare their hearts. It is very sad that many churches today encourage informal chat before the service in order to make the place of worship appear more welcoming. A warm welcome may be accomplished by a friendly greeting on the way in, but once seated, uninhibited conversation between worshippers is harmful to reverence and respect for the Lord. An organ played quietly, with people either praying or reading the Bible or a hymnbook, is impressive to outsiders who are helped by the prevailing reverence.

Some churches have tried to cure pre-service chatter by introducing a chorus or hymn sing-song, which seems to this writer to be a disastrous cure, not least because it usually marks the beginning of contemporary worship.

In these days of informality, stewarding has largely fallen out of use in churches, but it has great value, and from *James 2.1-3* appears to have been employed in New Testament gatherings. It deserves serious consideration today, especially by larger congregations. A sense of order and significance is at once evident in a stewarded church, and in such a church worship quickly takes on the character of a special occasion.

At the close of a service, after the closing prayer or benediction, the people should continue for a short time in undisturbed silent prayer. The one leading the worship should not 'dismiss' the congregation, instantly terminating the worship, and signalling the commencement of loud interaction between the people. Reverence in the house of God not only makes a powerful impression upon unconverted people, but it helps the sincerity and earnestness of believers.

CHAPTER 8

What Really Happened at Corinth?

How is it then, brethren? when ye come together, every one of you hath a psalm, hath a doctrine, hath a tongue, hath a revelation, hath an interpretation. Let all things be done unto edifying (1 Corinthians 14.26).

WHAT DO we make of Paul's description of a worship service in *1 Corinthians 14.26*? This verse, and those following, are pivotal to understanding worship. Should worship be reverent and ordered, or should it be characterised by informality, exuberance, spontaneity and innovation? This passage provides the answer.

Advocates of new-style worship claim that Paul provides here a picture of worship which is totally informal and uninhibited. They imagine that many people contributed, and different gifts were exercised. Promoters of contemporary worship are very pleased that many churches are now veering away from the formal, orderly style which has dominated the Bible-loving scene for generations. The traditional way of worship (they say) is straitjacketed, restricting a service to a very limited number of components, while the new style is unfettered and open to the 'flow' of the Spirit – just like (they think) the services at Corinth. And if one looks superficially and carelessly at the key verse it may indeed seem to speak of greater liberty and multiple contributions. 'How is it then, brethren?' asks Paul, 'when ye come together, *every one* of you hath a psalm, hath a doctrine, hath a tongue, hath a revelation, hath an interpretation.'

The first matter to be noted is that there is only one type of musical item in the Corinthian list and that is the singing of psalms. This should hardly encourage contemporary worship which is entirely built around musical performance. The early church had nothing like today's groups and orchestras, choirs and solos, ministers of music and song leaders.

That aside, there is a massive flaw in the idea that informal and uninhibited worship is described by Paul. The key to understanding the passage is the question – to whom is Paul speaking in this chapter? Is he speaking to the entire church, or to the leaders? A wrong interpretation assumes he is speaking to the whole church, in which case a very large number of people could be participating. But the reality is that he is speaking only to the appointed *leaders* of the church (to those possessing revelatory and teaching gifts), who had the responsibility of arranging worship. These are the people to whom he says – 'Every one of you hath a psalm, hath a doctrine . . .' The elders and prophets are in view. How can we be sure of this? The first decisive factor is the large size of the church at Corinth. It would not have been possible for all or even many of the people to contribute to a worship service. For this reason Paul's 'every one of you' could only be addressed to the leaders.

Furthermore, Paul severely restricts his 'every one of you' in verse 34, saying – 'Let your women keep silence in the churches.' If no woman could contribute, Paul's 'every one of you' must have been addressed to the leaders only.

How many prophets were there at Corinth? We are not told, but in *Acts 13* we have a snapshot of the church at Antioch, possibly of similar size, and we find there were only five prophets and teachers in that church, and this number was reduced when God by the Holy Spirit told them to send two on missionary service (Saul and Barnabas), leaving only three serving as prophets or teachers. We see from this that there were not many prophets and teachers even in very large churches. The picture of free-for-all, open, informal worship of an exuberant kind slowly crumbles when we examine the details.

It should not surprise us to find Paul specifically addressing the leaders of the Corinthian church in chapter fourteen, because at the end of chapter twelve he talks about apostles, prophets and teachers in the church. He then digresses into the beautiful and challenging thirteenth chapter about love, and then in chapter fourteen very logically continues to focus on prophets, teachers and tongues-speakers.

At Corinth there was clearly a degree of disorder on the 'platform'. Teachers, prophets and tongues-speakers (who were 'junior' prophets) were too eager to press forward with a contribution. To correct this, the platform party were given inspired rules that strictly limited the number of contributors. The resulting ordering of a service in *1 Corinthians 14* supports the traditional worship of Bible believers, which is reverent, orderly, structured and properly led by appointed pastors or elders. It does not endorse the modern innovative entertainment style of worship.

It is not always appreciated just how much Paul has to say about the right style of worship in *1 Corinthians 14*. Four very powerful words appear in this chapter, laying down the Lord's commands for harmonious and structured worship. The first word is in *1 Corinthians 14.33* – 'For God is not the author of confusion, but of peace, as in all churches of the saints.' If the reader has in mind the erroneous view that Paul has just charged the entire congregation with disorderly worship it may appear that he is correcting clamour and commotion, but that is not what he means. The Greek word translated 'confusion' describes disorder, where people act on their own, and not according to rules or expected order. It is the negative form of the verb 'to place down' or appoint. Paul is saying that God is *not* the author of worship that is not *placed down,* or arranged and appointed. In other words he instructs the Corinthian leaders to have an ordered, thoughtful, led approach.

This verse reproves service leaders who make things up as they go along. It also discourages a service in which numerous people give unpremeditated contributions.* Only a thoughtful approach includes in a service all the vital elements of worship outlined in Scripture, such as objective praise, subjective thanksgiving, repentance and affirmation and dedication.

The second key worship word in *1 Corinthians 14* is 'peace'. Paul says – 'For God is not the author of confusion, but of *peace.*' The *peace* word used here refers to reconciliation and harmony, being derived from the verb 'to join'. It shows that the component parts of the service must not be discordant, but fit well together, so that the service is *harmonious,* not a collection of unconnected fragments. This does not necessarily mean that we organise a *thematic* service, in which every hymn, reading and prayer features the theme soon to be presented in the sermon. It means that all the biblical components of worship combine to form a comprehensive whole. Does the service combine worthy praise, prayer, and the reading and proclamation of God's Word? Does it provide understanding, exhortation, comfort, and uplift for the people of God? Has there been a place for intercession? All these elements should surely be represented in a 'joined-together' service. This, says Paul, is what the Lord requires. This is not achieved when the service is built around the demands

---

* There is, of course, a notable exception to this. A church's 'domestic' prayer meeting will call for many contributions of prayer which will not have been prearranged, except for the announcing of topics for prayer. Hopefully, the hymns, Scripture reading and exhortation will have been prearranged by the chairman, but in any case the prayer meeting of the local church has a special warrant of its own in the New Testament. (See *The Power of Prayer Meetings,* Peter Masters, a *Sword & Trowel* booklet.)

of entertainment and music. We usually find such services have skipped Bible reading, and have nothing more than brief and superficial prayer.

The third significant worship word in *1 Corinthians 14* appears in verse 40 – 'Let all things be done *decently*.' The Greek word literally means 'well formed'. One modern translation says 'properly', and another, 'fitting'. In other words, a service must be well shaped, and appropriate for its purpose, confirming and consolidating the previous point. A service must be well formed in the sense of being balanced and well proportioned. We may imagine a potter working on a lump of clay, shaping it with his hands as the table rotates. He has a clear idea of how to achieve a well-formed item of pottery. He does not make either the top or the base too large. All is properly balanced. A service of worship should not only contain all the right components, but these must be present in the right proportion. The service is not an entertainment, but a balance of intelligent spiritual themes. Paul's word also means that the service must be *appropriate* for sacred things, not more suited to worldly and profane things. It is not appropriate to use the rhythms of the nightclub or the dance floor in the worship of God, nor is it appropriate for a worship leader to behave as a theatrical master of ceremonies. These things are not fitting.

The fourth important worship word is also in verse 40. Paul says, 'Let all things be done decently and *in order*.' This is a powerful term speaking again of the need for a regular arrangement or order in a service. When the Greek term is applied to an army, it refers to the fixed arrangement of men in ranks, formations, and battle dispositions, according to the plans of the generals. In *Luke 1.8* the word is used to describe how Zacharias diligently carried out his Temple duties in accordance with the prescribed sequence.

Order in worship means that services are arranged according to the rules and pattern of the Bible. Obviously the word must not be pressed to the point of absurdity, for the apostles did not read manuscripted sermons, or write liturgies. However, *order* tells us that a congregation gladly embraces and submits to a style of worship given by God. Innovation and gimmickry are out, along with exhibitionism and entertainment. Reverence is in, with all the components of worship which our Heavenly General requires. 'Order' spells obedience to God. It also entails predictability, an inevitable component of order.

These four terms prove that a service of worship should be well planned, containing all the vital elements of worship, being well proportioned, and in conformity with God's standards. The undirected spontaneity and exuberance claimed by new worship advocates is not found in *1 Corinthians 14*, which is all about reverence, thoughtfulness and obedience to God's directions. True power and glory is to be found in the joyous praise of believers who worship the Lord in his chosen way.

CHAPTER 9

Why Raise Hands?

IF THE LORD wants worship to be offered in spirit and in truth, why do many Christians find it necessary to employ hands, arms and body movements in order to get into a worshipping vein? Why do they have this urge to get the physical dimension in at all costs? Are they not trying to work up emotions and feelings by human means, rather than by thoughtful, spiritual worship? In this short chapter we look at the claim that raising of hands is sanctioned in the Bible and should therefore have its place in worship today. It is true there are several references to it in the *Psalms*, and one reference in the New Testament, but these have no connection with corporate worship, as we will show, and are wrenched out of context by charismatic teachers. Common sense should tell us it is highly unlikely that the Lord would require hand-raising in his church, contradicting his 'spirit and truth' rule.

Why, then, did David raise his hands, as recorded in *Psalm 28.2*: 'Hear the voice of my supplications ... when I lift up my hands toward thy holy oracle'? The answer is that David was far away from Jerusalem, probably escaping from Absalom. As an absentee, in his personal devotions he lifted up his hands toward the place of sacrifice in Jerusalem in order to identify with the offering up of the sacrifice by the priest. He could not be present, but he felt the need to express his solidarity with the offering. It is important to recognise that he would not have done this had he been present in Jerusalem, and able to attend the house of God, for only the priests offered up the sacrifices. His raising of hands was a symbolic act of identification on the part of an absent individual. It was not ordinarily done by the 'laity' in worship.

In *Psalm 63.4* David says: 'I will lift up my hands in thy name.' On this occasion he was in the wilderness of Judah and again isolated from the place of sacrifice. He longed to be in the sanctuary, and says so (verse 2). At the time of the sacrifice, he once again raised his hands to identify with the nightly offering.

In *Psalm 141.2* David is very clear on the matter. Being far from the Tabernacle yet again, he asked that his prayer would rise up like incense '. . . and the lifting up of my hands as the evening sacrifice'.

This action is not recorded anywhere in the Old Testament as a normal congregational activity, but a personal gesture having limited and specific significance. The question is – should we do the same as David? The obvious answer is – of course not, because the sacrifices are now finished. Our Lord and Saviour has fulfilled all the sacrificial laws and symbols, and they have ceased. That is why in the New Testament there is no instruction to literally raise our hands in worship. To do so (in the way David did) would revive the performance of the sacrifices and detract from the great sacrifice offered once for all, on Calvary's cross.

Today people do not raise their hands as David did, to identify with the oblation, but to obtain some kind of feeling or sense of contact with God, something that cannot be achieved by physical means.

Three other psalms mention actions with the hands, but these refer to other matters. *Psalm 119.48* speaks of lifting up hands to denote obedience to God, just as a workman would take up his tools. *Psalm 134.2* refers to the priests literally offering up sacrifices, and *Psalm 143.6* sees David figuratively (not literally) stretching forth his hands to God, as a needy child reaches out to its mother.

When Paul *(1 Timothy 2.8)* commands Christians to pray 'lifting up holy hands', he undoubtedly means this figuratively. To offer clean hands to God in a literal way, like little children showing parents that they have washed before a meal, would be an absurd thing to do. Christians are to lift up holy hands in their minds, meaning they should strive for holiness before they pray. The figure most likely comes from *Psalm 24.3-4* – 'Who shall ascend into the hill of the Lord? or who shall stand in his holy place? He that hath clean hands, and a pure heart.'

Raising of hands is just another example of a charismatic activity based on the flimsy misuse of Bible texts. As carried out today, hand-raising is an unbiblical human device, intended to help people to get into a mildly trance-like state of worked up emotions. It is done contrary to the 'spirit and truth' principle, and rather than helping real devotion it draws into the heart a taste for physical display in worship.

CHAPTER 10

Why Sing Hymns?

WHY DO WE sing hymns? Who invented the hymn? Long before the outstanding seventeenth and eighteenth-century hymnwriters, there were Reformation-period hymns. But the hymns of the Reformation were not the first, nor were the preceding Latin hymns, or even older Saxon hymns, the root source of the hymn. To find the first Christian hymns, we go right back to the pages of the New Testament, where the 'new song' is revealed.

In previous chapters we looked for guidance on worship in *Revelation* chapters four and five. None of that material will be repeated here, except to remind readers that these chapters provide a vision of the Church universal worshipping God. In reading the words of the 'new song' sung in these chapters it strikes us immediately that they are not words found in the *Psalms*. For example, we read of how the living creatures and the four and twenty elders fell down before the Lamb and –

'sung a new song, saying, Thou art worthy to take the book, and to open the seals thereof: for thou wast slain, and hast redeemed us to God by thy blood out of every kindred, and tongue, and people, and nation.'

What do the worshippers sing about in this new song? They sing most explicitly about Christ, and how he will unseal the book and work out the mighty purposes of God. They sing very specifically about Calvary, and we notice that they sing about it in the past tense. They sing in New Testament language about redemption by blood. They also sing about Gentile salvation, and again they sing in the past tense, of an accomplished event. They mention the conversion of the Gentiles out of every land and nation. They go on to make specific mention of the priesthood of all believers, and again they sing of this as an accomplished thing. They say that Christ – 'hast made us unto our God kings and priests: and we shall reign on the earth.' They sing about a future reign of Christ. And in *Revelation 5.12*, we find them again proclaiming the Lamb as the One who *was* slain. He is now risen again, and on the throne. Incarnation, crucifixion, resurrection and ascension are looked back on, and made the central and strongest elements in their worship. The Lamb is repeatedly named. The new song is all about things that have happened, and Christ Jesus (incarnate, crucified and risen from the dead) is the focus of their joy.

The new song is chiefly focused on things now fulfilled, through the work of Christ. The cherubim of justice and the mighty angelic host join the Church of both the Old and New Testament to sing this new song. The new hymn is a shining reflection of New Testament light, and we are compelled to ask: if it is right to sing such songs in Heaven, how can it be wrong to sing them on earth? But in any case, correct exegesis sees this vision as already describing the worship of the redeemed on earth, as well as in Heaven, throughout the Gospel age. For this reason we hold that Scripture requires us to sing hymns based on New Testament events, in addition to psalms. We are the Church of Jesus Christ, and he must be extolled by name and by explicit reference to his work in our hymns.

This writer has the greatest respect for those who hold that only the psalms of the Old Testament should be sung in church, and for many of our finest theological authors, past and present, including giants of faith and scholarship, who advocate psalms only. Nevertheless, I believe (with the majority of Bible believers) that they are greatly mistaken in saying that there is no scriptural warrant for singing hymns. On the contrary, the New Testament requires us to honour Christ by name in all things.

Certainly we should sing Old Testament psalms, but when we do so it is often necessary to adapt them to New Testament language. When C. H. Spurgeon compiled a psalter for his hymnbook he entitled it, *Spirit of the Psalms*, because most of the psalms were adapted to express New Testament revelation. The words of Isaac Watts (in his introduction to his hymnal of 1718) provide a famous statement of how the psalms ought best to be sung. He wrote –

> 'My design is to accommodate the **Book of Psalms** to Christian worship. In order to do this, it is necessary to divest David, Asaph, etc, of every other character but that of a psalmist and a saint, and to make them always speak the language of a Christian. Where the psalmist uses sharp invectives against his enemies, I have endeavoured to turn the edge of them against *our* spiritual adversaries – sin, Satan and temptation. Where the original runs in the form of prophecy concerning Christ and his salvation, it is not necessary that we should sing in the style of prediction when the things foretold are brought into open light by a full accomplishment.
>
> 'Where the psalmist speaks of the pardon of sin, I have added the merits of a Saviour. Where he talks of sacrificing goats or bullocks, I rather chose to mention the sacrifice of Christ. Where he promises abundance of wealth, honour, and long life, I have changed some of these typical blessings for grace, glory and life eternal. And I am fully satisfied that more honour is done to our blessed Saviour by spreading his name, his graces and actions in his own language, and according to the brighter revelations he has now made, than by going back again to the language of types and figures.'

Says Watts in effect – 'We have no need to sing in the language of prediction when the things foretold have been brought into the open light of day by their fulfilment. We should not limit our worship to the language of Old Testament types and shadows, never daring to mention the glorious truths of which they spoke.' Of course, many psalms contain theology and sentiments that transcend both Testaments, and very fine metrical versions of these exist which should also be sung.

Traditional hymns are rooted in the 'new song' of the closing book of the Bible, where the symbolised Church of all ages raises in Heaven the pattern for those who worship the Lamb until he returns, and then for ever.

CHAPTER 11

Seven Standards for Worthy Hymns

WHAT IS so special about our existing traditional-format hymns? Should they be defended and kept in use, or should they be replaced by modern-format alternatives? If they are to be retained, strong and compelling reasons must be given. This chapter will mention some of the high standards generally honoured by traditional hymns. To be welcome, new compositions must surely measure up to the standards of the past, which choruses and songs of new-style worship generally fail to do. But how shall we define or determine what is a good hymn? Here are seven qualities which the writer believes are the necessary minimum standards, all of which have been achieved by many well-accepted traditional hymnwriters.

1 The first standard for a worthy hymn is that it should reflect the example and method of the *Psalms* – the Old Testament hymn-book inspired by God. The *Psalms* should shape hymns of human composition in a number of ways. Hymns should honour and imitate the topics represented in the *Psalms*, and the balance of

worship components. (See the charts at the end of this chapter.)

Perhaps the greatest point of departure from traditional hymns in new-style worship is the abandonment of the principles of the *Psalms.* Contemporary worship songs certainly employ selected psalms, but in their new lyrics abandon the 'intellectual' level of the psalms, along with their dignity, reverence, weighty character, style of worship, and range of doctrines.

2 The second standard for a worthy hymn is that it will edify the worshipper; that is, it will add something to him. It will, perhaps, expound and apply the Word to his heart, giving the opportunity for a heartfelt response to God for what has been understood. Like a psalm, it will be profound, yet available to everyone's understanding. It will have broad scope and stretch the soul, yet it will never be too complex for the average mind. This is the standard of the *Psalms,* neither too high, nor too low (unlike modern compositions that are usually too low).

A worthy hymn will have the capacity to throw light on scriptural truth. The hymns of Watts and Wesley educated countless people, from farmhands to royals, in great Christian doctrines. Unlike modern lyrics, they explored great doctrines and helped develop profound believers. They frequently taught the principles of trust and devotion especially in trial, hymnwriter John Newton being among the chief authors of experiential worship. The question proposed by Paul, 'Does it edify?' applies to the hymn. What exactly has it accomplished? Has it added to our understanding, or our godliness? Has it built us up, not just at an emotional level, but at a truly spiritual level?

3 The third standard for a worthy hymn is that it will be reverent, especially in addressing the *mighty* God. It will not be merely sentimental. It will not treat God as a mate living next door. It will have reverence, calling upon the One who is high and lifted up. It will assume a humble attitude before the God of holiness and authority. It

will not rush into the divine presence without repentance. It will not make demands on God or sing banal and repetitive lyrics that bring the maker of Heaven and earth down to the level of the kindergarten.

4 The fourth standard for a worthy hymn is that it will be doctrinally clear, not ambiguous or vague. Strange as it may sound, a worthy hymn will be clear enough to offend wilful unbelievers. If a hymn is so innocuous that universal acceptance is assured, then it clearly misses the mark. If writers manage to speak so vaguely and so generally that people of every religious hue are at ease, they cannot be producing hymns of worthy clarity. If they satisfy all theological positions at once, how can they expand the understanding of the worshipper? It is significant that the best-known contemporary songs are immensely popular with theological liberals, and also with Catholic congregations throughout the world.

The effect of vague, vapid choruses and hymns is also extremely damaging to a sound congregation, because people become trained to worship in a lightweight manner with only half their minds, and half their sincerity and earnestness. If we want a congregation to sing with sustained understanding and earnestness, then the hymns must have theological substance.

5 The fifth standard for a worthy hymn is that it should avoid over-ornamental lines, and not suffocate its sentiments with excessive embellishments, so that worshippers cannot sing with the understanding (1 Corinthians 14.15). Good hymnwriters have usually commanded a wide vocabulary, but have clearly disciplined their words in order to be understood. The secular poet may be free to indulge himself and exhibit his powers, but the hallmark of great hymns is their combination of depth and clarity.

6 A sixth standard for a worthy hymn is that it will have a good structure and sensible rhyming, the technical part of hymn-writing. A quality hymn does not have forced or 'near miss' rhymes. Lesser hymns betray the struggles of their authors in this respect.

The first or second lines evidently worked well, but then the author ran into difficulty and had to bludgeon words around to create a rhyme. Sometimes sense and logic have yielded to the need for a rhyming word. The gifted hymnwriter seldom reflects this difficulty. His or her structure is consistent and line of thought seamless. The high pinnacle of hymnwriting is seen when a hymn holds and builds its theme through the verses. The author is not forced to keep changing the subject because he could not maintain the metre or rhyming with the topic he began with. Poorer hymns jump around so much there is often a change of theme in every line. The mind of the worshipper is torn from one unexpected (and unconnected) idea to another, and so he gives up tracking the sense and sings with little earnestness. The hymn is a bag of fragments.

The work of identifying sentiments, arranging them in a logical and developing order, is commonly accomplished in traditional hymnody, whereas contemporary songs, by comparison, fail constantly. If we define a hymn by the standards achieved in the past, there are very few hymns being written today.

7 The seventh standard for a worthy hymn is that it should be free from mystical statements. Hymns are bound to have an element of this, because it is not possible to express some of the wonderful things of the faith without using terms and figures which, if subjected to scrutiny, do not entirely fit reality. We speak, for example, of 'knowing the Lord', but there may not be space in a hymn to define carefully what is meant, or to introduce the 'by faith' concept. Contemporary worship songs teem with mystical sentiments.

These points are offered chiefly to show that the traditional hymn was never an accident or quirk of culture. Able writers thought about what they were doing. They possessed the ability to handle hymn composition, and they honoured the essential principles of worship.

Weaknesses in traditional hymns

All that glitters is not gold, and it must be acknowledged that there are verses in the corpus of traditional-style hymns that cry out for correction. Just as it is not necessary that we should sing in the language of the Old Testament, so also it is not necessary that we should be tied to the language of the seventeenth and eighteenth centuries. Hymns need not have a dusty, ancient image. Worshippers should not have to 'translate' into modern speech as they sing. Some traditional hymns are marred by gruesomely old-fashioned expressions, and these need editorial help. This is not about 'Thees and Thous', which in the view of this writer continue to be a valid form of respectful address to Almighty God. This is about quaint and awkward words and lines.

It is well known that Charles Wesley's great hymn – 'Hark! the herald angels sing' – began life in 1739 as 'Hark, how all the welkin rings'. We are glad that this received very early attention. By 1753 George Whitefield's *Collection* had altered it to the present famous first line (the change coming after only 14 years). The same hymn benefitted from other early alterations. Martin Madan's hymnbook of 1760 introduced the line 'With th'angelic host proclaim', in place of 'Universal nature sang'. In 1807 the *New Version* Anglican psalter and hymnbook added the refrain. Many other hymns have been similarly improved by editing, and the process needs to go on. We are now separated from Watts and Wesley by well over two centuries.

The twentieth-century era of hymnbooks produced by mainline denominations inflicted some injury to hymns. Prior to this there were numerous fine hymns expressing the doctrines of grace, and many hymns about conversion and Christian experience, but as the denominations became dominated by liberal theology, hymns that were too explicit in expressing a doctrinal position were either omitted, or their distinctive theology was edited out. Non-evangelical hymns crept in. These have done much to tarnish the image of the traditional hymn genre. Nevertheless, there remains intact a vast and magnificent storehouse of biblical praise in traditional hymns, which have been a vehicle of sincere praise to God for millions of Christian people.

The philosophers of Athens in Paul's day spent their time listening for some new thing to arrive in the theatre of thought. In our day we are often obsessed with the idea that new is good and old is bad. But we believe new compositions should surely follow the standards of the traditional.

THE PSALMS

as a guide to worship, analysed to show
proportions of different aspects of worship

ALL CATEGORIES OF PSALM – OBJECTIVE OR PERSONAL?

	Objective*		Personal	
Psalms of praise, thanksgiving, affirmation or reflection	70	**47%**	18	**12%**
Petitions	21	**14%**	41	**27%**
Total:	91	**61%**	59	**39%**

*ie: focusing either on God, or on themes outside oneself

PSALMS OF PRAISE

CHIEF SUBJECT:

God; his acts in general; creation and the natural world	28	**19%**
Reflecting on the human race (generally negatively)	13	**9%**
Reflection and thanksgiving for own experience	18	**12%**
Reflecting on redemption in general	29	**19%**

PETITIONAL PSALMS – some psalms divide over two categories

For deliverance and upholding	19	**13%**
Repentance	11	**7%**
Longing for assurance	9	**6%**
Commitment/dedication	7	**5%**
Sanctification	7	**5%**
For Israel (ie: for the deliverance and advancement of the church)	11	**7%**
For judgement upon enemies (Some in which the good of the church is the objective, and some in which the psalmist is a type of Christ acting in divine judgement.)	9	**6%**

THE PSALMS

*Categories of worship in the Psalms compared with a
sample traditional hymnbook*

	The Book of Psalms	A Traditional Hymnbook
Psalms of praise, thanksgiving, affirmation or reflection	88 **59%**	328 **56%** hymns
Psalms of petition (asking psalms)	62 **41%**	257 **44%** hymns

*A comparison of petitional psalms with a traditional
hymnbook (taking hymns other than psalm-based hymns)*

	The Book of Psalms	A Traditional Hymnbook
Repentance	11 **7%**	48 **8%**
Israel/church	11 **7%**	46 **8%**
Commitment	7 **5%**	31 **5%**
Deliverance and upholding	19 **13%**	81 **13%**

It will be noticed that the selection of hymns in an analysed
typical traditional hymnbook relates remarkably closely to the
Book of Psalms, showing the influence of the Psalter on generations of hymnwriters. Several hymnbooks of a conservative and
reformed kind appear to be very similar in composition.

CHAPTER 12

Reverence Begins in the Place of Worship

NO ONE would deny that reverence is due to Almighty God by right. But how can the Lord be properly acknowledged and worshipped if the worshipper has replaced him with a god of his own making, a much smaller god? Today many evangelical Christians have remodelled God, turning him into a being only a bit higher than themselves. He is no longer treated as the infinite, almighty, holy God, who sees and searches every heart. He is merely a chum or pal sharing our smallness and triviality, and enjoying our entertainment-based culture. He is no longer to be given maximum respect and reverence.

With this new god, Moses would not need to remove the shoes from his feet, nor the apostle John fall at his feet as dead. This revised god does not mind how we worship him, and so we need have no inhibitions or qualms about anything we do in his presence. But to change God is to deny him and to insult him. So where is reverence today? Where is the God of Elijah? Where is Old Testament Jehovah?

Where is the mighty God so respectfully addressed in the recorded prayers of the New Testament? Amazingly, this glorious God is not wanted, even by many who believe his Word and seek his salvation. Reverence has become distasteful. It has been relegated to the debris of a cast-off former culture. 'Give us a God,' people seem to cry, 'on our level.'

This chapter is about the necessity of reverence for God and how also it brings great benefits and blessings to worshippers. *Hebrews 12.28-29* provides a specially challenging verse for the present day:

> 'Wherefore we receiving a kingdom which cannot be moved, let us have grace, whereby we may serve God acceptably with reverence and godly fear: for our God is a consuming fire.'

'Reverence' here literally means – with downcast eyes or great humility. 'Fear' means caution, or holy fear.

The Lord Jesus himself, when living out for us a life of perfect righteousness, maintained the deepest reverence toward the Father, the Bible telling us that his prayers were heard because he 'feared', using this same Greek term for caution or reverence *(Hebrews 5.7)*. The term 'fear', indicating reverential fear, appears often in the New Testament. Cornelius of Caesarea, visited by Peter, was acknowledged by all to be one who 'feared' God. His reverence for God was conspicuous. When preaching at Antioch in Pisidia, Paul appealed twice to those that 'feared' God, using the same reverential fear term. They would be the people who truly received the Word. 'Fear God!' wrote Peter, using the same term *(1 Peter 2.17)*. 'Fear God!' said the angel of the preaching of the everlasting Gospel in *Revelation*, using the same term, indicating that the ultimate objective of the Gospel is to bring men and women not just to salvation, but to reverence *(Revelation 14.7)*.

The victorious people of God sang, 'Who shall not fear thee, O Lord, and glorify thy name?' using the same reverential fear term *(Revelation 15.4)*. And the voice from the throne of God commanded, 'Praise our God, all ye his servants, and ye that fear him, both small and great' *(Revelation 19.5).*

In the parable of the wicked husbandmen, the Lord spoke of a householder who let out his property, but when he sent servants to receive the produce, they were beaten and killed and stoned. Finally the householder sent his son saying, 'They will reverence my son.' Reverence, respect and deference is exactly what is due to the eternal Son of God, the Lord of glory. Its expression is to be seen first and foremost in worship, and if it is not there, it will not be seen in other areas of the Christian life either. Reverence-deficient worship soon leads to Christians being shallow in commitment, seriousness, depth and even holiness. Reverence in worship is paramount for believers, and must be firmly maintained.

Another very valuable passage about reverence is *1 Timothy 4.7-9,* where Paul says to Timothy:

> 'Exercise thyself rather unto godliness. For bodily exercise profiteth little: but godliness is profitable unto all things.'

To show the pivotal importance of these words Paul attaches the comment, 'This is a faithful saying and worthy of all acceptation.' He is talking about the necessity of reverence toward God. We may think that the key word in these verses – *godliness* – refers in a general way to righteous character. Paul's exhortation then would mean, 'Exercise yourself in sanctified living.' This, of course, would be a correct thing to do, but the word *godliness* does not mean that. It is a highly special word with a very distinctive meaning. The Greek is *eusebeia,* meaning 'well-devout'. It refers to our entire attitude toward God. It is far more specific than righteousness, and as this is so important we shall briefly prove the point by glancing at other passages where the word is used.

In *1 Timothy 6.11* we see a very interesting construction: 'But thou, O man of God, flee these things; and follow after righteousness, GODLINESS, faith, love, patience, meekness.' Here godliness sits among other specific qualities. Like them, it is distinctive. It is obviously not a general term for Christian living as it takes its place in a list of very particular virtues. The term is used in the same way in the famous 'list' of *2 Peter 1.5-7* – 'And beside this, giving all diligence, add to your faith virtue; and to virtue knowledge; and to knowledge temperance; and to temperance patience; and to patience GODLINESS; and to godliness brotherly kindness; and to brotherly kindness charity.' Godliness again sits as a specific virtue alongside others.

The Greek word in question appears in classical literature where philosophers used it to mean *an appropriate attitude toward the gods.* This is the sense in the epistles, where the word indicates a right demeanour before God, that is, reverence and respect. It is all about the fear of God, humility before God, and deference toward God.

The root of all our problems today as evangelical Christians is the collapse of such reverence. With the new style of worship, all carefulness in God's presence and all deep respect for him has gone, and yet this is the ultimate purpose of salvation – to revere and obey him. Paul therefore says, 'Exercise yourself unto reverence.' Other spiritual graces cannot flourish without this foundation.

Many believers exclaim – 'Oh, but I want to have joy and happiness and the filling of the Spirit. I want a thrilling sense of God and of glory.' Such a desire is fine, but it can only come with reverence. God must always be to us a great God, to whom we come with reverence and submission. It is only when we truly hold God in respect that the Holy Spirit gives genuine Christian joy. If we have no taste for reverence we are in spiritual trouble, and only able to achieve a sham, worked-up, shallow, emotional substitute. All the charismatic meetings in the world, with their noise, rhythm and sensationalism, cannot manufacture *real* Christian joy, if they do not have a foundation of reverence and awe.

The prime movers of contemporary worship, with its love of entertainment-style music and its typical shallowness, generally show the same indifference to reverence in their manner of leading worship. They run jauntily on to their platform like stage or television celebrities projecting their personalities, and behaving in an entirely flippant and irreverent manner in the presence of the holy, all-powerful and wonderful God. Reverence knows how to honour divine dignity, but for them it is burdensome, restrictive and irrelevant.

As it happens, reverence is a door to much blessing in this present life, as well as in eternity, as Paul says in *1 Timothy 4.7-8*. So, he exhorts, 'exercise thyself...unto godliness.' The word *godliness*, as we have shown, refers to reverence and respect for God. The Greek word translated 'exercise' is literally *gymnasticise*. So Paul says – gymnasticise yourself to practise reverence.

There is no doubt that reverence is instinctual for newborn Christians. When we are converted, our new nature is impregnated with great respect for God, but we can allow this to run down, and even lose it. Therefore, says Paul, it must be exercised. In the physical realm exercise does not create muscles, but it certainly develops and preserves them. Similarly, reverence comes with the new nature, but exercise is necessary to strengthen and maintain it.

The apostle Paul does not scorn bodily exercise when he says, 'For bodily exercise profiteth little.' Some believe he means, that it profits only for a little time. However, the statement may equally be understood as – 'For bodily exercise profits *to a* little.' Paul knew, of course, that an athlete's physical training would not necessarily help him control his temper, or any other sin-tendency. Physical exercise works only in a limited area. The apostle's point is that the exercise of reverence has a much broader benefit, because it deepens and strengthens every aspect of a Christian's life and service, and prepares him for eternity. 'For bodily exercise profiteth *[to a]* little: but godliness *[or reverence]* is profitable unto all things, having promise of the life that now is, and of that which is to come.'

If worship is stripped of reverence, then reverence will be stunted in all other aspects of Christian living. What begins in worship, spreads into the whole Christian life. If worship is more like a performance, with showing off, imitation of the world, sensation-seeking, much noise, and everything for my pleasure, then the Christian life will follow suit. How cruel it is, then, for churches to abandon reverent worship, for believers will be seriously hurt and disadvantaged in their personal spiritual lives.

Take our understanding of the Bible. Reverence for God produces humility and fear of offending him in the handling of the Bible. 'This is God's sacred Word,' we think. 'I must not rush through it. I must open my heart day by day to what God is saying. I must make sure I get it right, and if I don't understand it, I must consult a reliable book or person for help. I must learn and obey.' Reverence leads to conscientiousness with Scripture, and this in turn leads to right understanding. Reverence certainly helps us not to come to hasty and superficial conclusions, safeguarding us against many errors. This attitude of reverence and care is seen perfectly in the stance of the apostle Peter, recorded in *2 Peter 1.19-21*:

> 'We have also a more sure word of prophecy; whereunto ye do well that ye take heed, as unto a light that shineth in a dark place, until the day dawn, and the day star arise in your hearts: knowing this first, that no prophecy of the scripture is of any private interpretation. For the prophecy came not in old time by the will of man: but holy men of God spake as they were moved by the Holy Ghost.'

The preacher who has reverence checks his preparatory work with conscientious care. If he thinks he sees in the text something he has not seen before, he worries lest his imagination should have led him astray, and checks his understanding more carefully. Reverence keeps him from falling into foolish conclusions and errors, checking his step and humbling his self-confidence. If reverence is omitted from worship, it is unlikely to be found in our handling of the Bible. The house of God is the best 'gymnasium' for reverence.

Turning from Bible study to holiness of life, reverence again makes all the difference, and strengthens our advance. Without reverence, repentance for sin becomes light and easy, but with it we become far more serious and determined.

In *2 Corinthians 7*, Paul speaks of the repentance of the Corinthians, saying, in effect, 'When you repented of sins you had committed, what heart-searching there was! What sensitivity of conscience there was! What hatred of yourselves was shown! What zeal and vehemence you had, to get rid of the wrong! You had such reverence for God, and awareness of his holiness, that you longed to be accepted before him, and you were really sorry and struggled to get this matter right.'

Reverence for God says, 'I *must* leave this sin behind. I *must* obtain his pardon and forgiveness before I proceed with anything, for God sees me!' Reverence gives birth to great diligence.

The believer may always run into the presence of God just as a child runs into the presence of a loving father, but not without reverence and respect, because our heavenly Father demands holiness, and is severe in his holy indignation against sin. Reverence will never erode our joy, but it will restrain us from collapsing into lightness and superficiality. Once again we may say, if reverence is not found in worship, it will not be present to help our advance in holiness. Reverence for God shapes our conduct before the watching world like no other influence. What is our deportment before unconverted people? What is our bearing, our stance and our behaviour? If we have deep reverence and respect for God, we will always feel ourselves to be 'on duty' as his servants. The last thing we will want to do is to let him down.

Reverence for God does not forget that he observes our every reaction to circumstances, and so we never abandon our composure and fall to bad behaviour. We are diligent to witness, and careful to control ourselves when under stress. Reverence always remembers that God knows best, and that he is providing for and training us for our eternal good. Reverence does not doubt the Lord, and cannot be bitter against him. It holds us through many a valley, and sees us through to new phases of joy and peace.

Reverence makes husbands and wives say to themselves, 'God has given me a lifelong partner and a charge to keep my marriage pure and harmonious and purposeful. Because this commission is from the mighty and eternal God whom I revere and adore, I will keep it with awe and diligence. I will keep alive the flame of love and the vision of marriage, and will behave with respect and affection in every situation.' It is reverence for God that causes us to subdue unworthy thoughts about one another, and practise appreciation.

Reverence for God holds us in obedience to the rules of the Christian life, for we know that he observes, chastises and rewards according to our conduct. Yet such reverence will not be found in us if it is not exercised and developed first in the time of worship.

In the light of all these things, how can reverence be exercised? One of the chief aspects of training in the physical sphere is *sacrifice* (as Paul shows). In sport a readiness to sacrifice drives all training, and the exercising of reverence to God necessitates self-denial. Certain things must be put aside. To purify worship, levity (but not joy) must be put aside, and with it emotional self-indulgence. The Lord must have highest place. If we are ready to do this, and to place God first and foremost in worship, then we will find no hardship in extending sacrifice to all of life. Some believers need to make a pledge to sacrifice worldliness. Reverence for God will cause us to say, 'I do not want an immoral culture to dominate and mould my thinking. I therefore sacrifice my worldly entanglements for the Lord's sake.'

Reverence also leads believers to consecrate their individual programmes to the Lord. They do not succumb to every activity open to them. Should friends come alongside and propose unfruitful activities, they pause, reflect and decline. If they yielded to every overture they would have no time for devotions, Christian service and other priorities.

This kind of discipline applies to worship in the house of God when novelties and gimmicks are proposed. It applies also to daily life. But we repeat yet again that this consecrated attitude to life is only found where believers have deep respect for God, and exercise reverence in worship.

An athlete also sacrifices liberty of dress, donning appropriate gear for training and competition, and, in a sense, so should we. The believer says, 'I will sacrifice the right to dress however I like whether in church or at business.' We may be under pressure in our environment to follow sensual styles, but we have a moral dress code to observe, and must stay within the bounds of modesty. Reverence for God leads to reverence for his tastes and standards, and we want to please him and live for him. It is not surprising that wherever reverence has been thrown out of worship, even the dress standards of believers have been lost also.

For some believers, it may be pleasurable superficiality that has to be curbed. They must pray, 'Lord, I sacrifice my desire to live in constant lightness.' Clearly this affects some people more than others, but some want to be superficial and insubstantial in behaviour all day long, and never serious. They must sacrifice their perverse escapism into whatever amuses, or their constant avoidance of disciplined and sustained thought. Such a pledge is the gymnastic training of reverence.

Every day the believer in training goes through a kind of programme check – What am I able to do for the Lord today? What will I do in my spare time? Should I visit someone, perhaps to draw back a faltering friend? Today I will serve and honour the Lord. If I find myself in trouble I will count my privileges and remember the promises. No matter what, I will respect sacred duties, and not skimp on devotions. I will remember that I represent the Lord in all situations.

Reverent Christians do not insist on having their own way all the time. They gladly submit to hard work in the Lord's service, and are sacrificial in their stewardship. Reverence to God influences all these things, and if it should be lost, we soon fall to superficial Christian living. How is our reverence? Have we missed this crucial department of the Christian life? As we have repeatedly asserted – reverence in worship is the essential starting point! Take that away (as contemporary worship music does) and there is no hope that we will even remotely resemble the kind of people whom God desires to be his own.

CHAPTER 13

Forfeiting the Soul of Evangelicalism

T HIS BOOK BEGAN with the assertion that worship is one of the most important issues confronting Bible churches today. Throughout the world contemporary Christian music has captured countless churches, absorbing them into the domain of semi-charismatic, worldly evangelicalism. Sometimes the preaching has largely remained sound, but for how long now that the worship ethos of such churches has so dramatically changed? Whether its victims realise it or not, the contemporary worship movement is the instrument of the hour to pull down both the conduct and the doctrinal walls of Zion. How the arch-enemy of the churches of Christ and of human souls will be straining to speed on such a catastrophe!

If we give new worship the smallest foothold it will ruin the highest activity entrusted to us, that is the reverent, intelligent and joyful offering of worthy spiritual praise. Many who began by singing one new worship song at every service, were soon singing two, then three, then the band and drums came in, and so on. It is very noticeable that wherever this worship has been embraced, worldliness and shallowness have followed, and a new generation has arisen that does not know the difference between the church and the world. It is obvious from the experience of many churches that new worship brings in wood, hay and stubble, grieving away the power of the Spirit to grant genuine conversions.

In this closing respectful appeal to spiritual under-shepherds and all believers, may I urge the consideration of several fearful outcomes. Even the partial adoption of contemporary worship will inevitably constitute a bridge to the total acceptance of 'Christian' rock culture. Composers and writers of 'sounder' modern genre songs say themselves that their primary aim is to draw conservative churches into the fold of Christian rock, and also to hasten ecumenical advance.

May I also warn that the adoption of contemporary worship will be an act of *pastoral insensitivity and cruelty* because it will destroy in the young all sense of separation from the world, delivering them into the power of secular culture. How can they be expected to keep their personal lives clear of sinful, worldly culture, if this is incorporated into the worship of their church? Never before have Bible-believing pastors and churches adopted anything as damaging.

With the adoption of contemporary worship, many more churches will dramatically change character in the years ahead. Where will *your* church be five or ten years from now? Will it become a lightweight, entertainment-based community, drinking from this world's fountains, and stripped of the behaviour and commitment of truly biblical Christianity? Will it have become a charismatic church, like so many, with worshippers either dancing or falling in the aisles? Will it be unrecognisable as a once conservative, Bible-obeying fellowship, distinctive from the world?

This surrender of Christian distinctives is already taking place with significant churches becoming 'new evangelical' and charismatic in towns and cities everywhere. May God help us to cherish and guard the great principles of worship expressed in his Word, rediscovered at the Reformation, and kept by millions over so many generations. May we prove the Lord in loyalty to him, and be faithful to our charge as pastors and church officers.

Scripture matters. Principles count. The Lord must be loved and observed in all things. Never let anyone take away biblical worship. Whatever the cost, hold on to the distinctive values honoured universally by all believers until recent decades, keeping worship untainted by the fleshly tastes and inventions of secular entertainment. Let us hold fast to these until the Great Day dawns, and the shadows flee away, and we look with rapture on our King, whose all-surpassing glory will be unobscured by the things of the world for all eternity.

More on Biblical Musical Instruments
Notes from Chapter 6: Brass, Strings and Percussion?

[1] *Psalm 5*, according to the Hebrew inscription, was to be accompanied by flutes, most likely a lone flute. This very plaintive psalm was sung on pilgrimage, and definitely not in the Tabernacle or Temple. It is an exceptional case where an instrument suitable to travel in the open was required.

[2] David's initial assembly of instruments for the first and disastrous recovery of the ark included timbrels or tambourines *(2 Samuel 6.5; 1 Chronicles 13.8)*. While the ark remained at the house of Obededom, David radically reformed and revised all the arrangements for its transportation to bring them into line with the law. At this time he was given (with Gad, the king's seer) new commands for musical instruments *(2 Chronicles 29.25)*. The timbrel was not now included, and never again appears in any list of instruments for direct or Temple worship. The second stage of the recovery of the ark (representing the ongoing rule) was accomplished without them.

[3] The history of the use of the trumpet in worship went back to *Numbers 10* where God commanded two silver trumpets for calling the people to the Tabernacle. The priests were to play them, and continued to do so in succeeding generations. They were to be blown on special feasts and at the beginning of months over the burnt offerings to remind the people of the

nature of their deliverance. They were never instruments for accompanying 'ordinary' worship. Generally, the number of trumpets used on special occasions continued to be two *(1 Chronicles 16.6)*. Exceptionally, 120 priests played trumpets at the consecration of Solomon's Temple. This was the largest crowd ever gathered for worship, and the largest and longest burning of offerings.

[4] What about Heman's horn in *1 Chronicles 25.5*? The three normal instruments are mentioned as a group twice. An odd-man-out reference to the horn appears in verse 5 – 'All these were the sons of Heman the king's seer ... to lift up the horn.' It is clear that this is a description of Heman alone, with one of three possible meanings. (1) It may refer to Heman being famous for once being selected to play a priest's trumpet *(1 Chronicles 16.42)*; (2) it may refer to his having been selected to sing a kingdom-extolling psalm; (3) it may have the meaning adopted by the *NIV*, which says that Heman's sons were given him by God 'to exalt him' – the horn being seen in a figurative light. A literal horn would flatly contradict all the other instrument lists in these chapters.

[5] The orchestra assembled to accompany the ark for the second stage of its recovery (an open-air procession) had three cymbals, eleven lyres and six harps. Once the ark was inside the tent the orchestra was reduced to eight lyres and harps, one cymbal and two trumpets. The size of the orchestra changed, but never the types of instrument. The restriction was maintained. In *1 Chronicles 25.1-7*, the total number of musicians was 288, of whom about 260 were in the choir, and these doubtless worked on some kind of rota.

[6] 'Synagogue' is really a New Testament word, but we use it here as a useful term for regional and district centres of worship – in other words, the Jewish local assembly (as in *Psalm 74.8*).

[7] In *Psalms 8, 81* and *84* the Hebrew inscription (though obscure) refers either to a harp, or is a direction of musical measure. The titles of a number of psalms include terms that do not refer to instruments, but to the mood, tone and measure of the psalm, and some are obscure. The Hebrew inscription meaning 'After lily of the testimony' occurs four times, and this is occasionally and controversially claimed to refer to trumpets because they have a lily shape. However, this is almost unthinkable because three of the four psalms in question are subdued prayers of tearful lamentation and pleading for help! More likely the 'lily' referred to a gentle style of music appropriate for a deeply touched heart.

[8] Some expositors say this speaks of both the earthly sanctuary *and* the wider firmament. In this case, this psalm is another which simply covers the whole spectrum of life – from Temple worship to civic and social life.

Psalms and Hymns of Reformed Worship
Editor: Peter Masters

Formatted for use in churches – 5½" x 7½" – printed in clear Roman typeface, hymns in two columns to the page, case-bound in blue, moisture-proof cloth with title in gold blocking.

This selection exploits the very best of all hymnwriters in the Reformation tradition, drawing no hymns from Catholic, liberal or charismatic sources. A number of 'lost' but strongly doctrinal and experimental hymns have been restored to use, the hymnbook including more hymns on response to the Gospel, and communion with Christ than in other collections. A careful ratio is maintained between objective and subjective hymns.

817 hymns, 226 of which are psalm versions, or evangelical versions of psalms, reverently updated wherever necessary to eliminate archaic language, and maintaining pronouns such as 'thee' and 'thou' only in addressing God.

The Charismatic Illusion
Co-author: John C. Whitcomb
100 pages, paperback, ISBN 978 1 908919 70 0

Now with more answers to questions asked by people investigating the arguments, this veteran book contends for the biblical position on the gifts that prevailed for nearly 2,000 years before the charismatic movement came along.

Here is the dynamic teaching of the Spirit that sustained true churches and believers through dark and bright years of history, through the Reformation, through the Puritan era, through the time of great Confessions of Faith, through repeated awakenings and revivals, and through the worldwide growth of the modern missionary movement.

Here is the case for authentic, biblical, spiritual life.

Steps for Guidance
In the Journey of Life
134 pages, paperback, ISBN 978 1 870855 66 2

In recent years the subject of how to find God's guidance has become controversial. Some say that God does not have a specific plan for the lives of his people, but allows us to please ourselves. Others say God's will is known by dreams, visions, and 'words of knowledge'.

By contrast with these sadly unbiblical ideas, this book presents the time-honoured, scriptural view that Christians must seek God's will in all the major decisions of life, such as career, marriage, location, and church. Six essential steps are traced from the Bible, and principles are given on additional practical issues such as possessions and leisure activities; ambition and wealth; joining or leaving a church. Here is a strong challenge to authentic Christian commitment, with an abundance of pastoral advice.

Faith, Doubts, Trials and Assurance
139 pages, paperback, ISBN 978 1 870855 50 1

Ongoing faith is essential for answered prayer, effective service, spiritual stability and real communion with God. In this book many questions are answered about faith, such as – How may we assess the state of our faith? How can faith be strengthened? What are the most dangerous doubts? How should difficult doubts be handled? What is the biblical attitude to trials? How can we tell if troubles are intended to chastise or to refine? What can be done to obtain assurance? What are the sources of assurance? Can a believer commit the unpardonable sin? Exactly how is the Lord's presence felt?

Dr Masters provides answers, with much pastoral advice, drawing on Scripture throughout.

The Lord's Pattern for Prayer
118 pages, paperback, ISBN 978 1 870855 36 5

Subtitled – 'Studying the lessons and spiritual encouragements in the most famous of all prayers.' This volume is almost a manual on prayer, providing a real spur to the devotional life. The Lord's own plan and agenda for prayer – carefully amplified – takes us into the presence of the Father, to prove the privileges and power of God's promises to those who pray.

Chapters cover each petition in the Lord's Prayer. Here, too, are sections on remedies for problems in prayer, how to intercede for others, the reasons why God keeps us waiting for answers, and the nature of the prayer of faith.

God's Rules for Holiness
Unlocking the Ten Commandments
139 pages, paperback, ISBN 978 1 870855 37 2

Taken at face value the Ten Commandments are binding on all people, and will guard the way to Heaven, so that evil will never spoil its glory and purity. But the Commandments are far greater than their surface meaning, as this book shows. They challenge us as Christians on a still wider range of sinful deeds and attitudes. They provide positive virtues as goals. And they give immense help for staying close to the Lord in our walk and worship.

The Commandments are vital for godly living and for greater blessing, but we need to enter into the panoramic view they provide for the standards and goals for redeemed people.

For a full listing of Wakeman titles please see www.wakemantrust.org